CREATE YOUR OWN NET WORTH

SUNDAY ADELAJA

Sunday Adelaja

CREATE YOUR OWN NET WORTH

©2017 Sunday Adelaja

ISBN 978-1-908040-30-5

Cover design by Alexander Bondaruk

Interior design by Olena Kotelnykova

CONTENTS

PREFACE

Our world is in a crisis. We are in a crisis involving the understanding of worth and net worth. Many people remain ignorant of their own worth, whilst arduously struggling to build a net worth.

This book will address the two dilemmas. It will give you an understanding of your worth, while taking you through the process of building your net worth. For only a person that knows his worth is confident enough to build a net worth for himself.

I am releasing this book as part of a fifty book collection to commemorate my 50th birthday anniversary. My personal journey has helped me realise that self-worth is at the basis of all achievements.

You need confidence to make incredible achievements in life. You especially need self-confidence to be able to create a net worth.

Every man has a worth but not every man has a net worth, worse still is the fact that most people are not aware that it is in their power to be able to create their own net worth. I therefore want to congratulate you, how wonderful it is that you are holding this book in your hands about to begin on an incredible journey!

Let the journey begin, the journey to discover your worth, the journey to create the skills that are needed to for you to create your own net worth. Let's change the world together.

For the Love of God, Church and Nation.

Dr. Sunday Adelaja.

INTRODUCTION

Many years ago, I decided to purchase a new shoe for myself so I went to one of the largest shopping malls within the city. On getting to the shopping mall, I went into one of the shops where shoes were being sold. When I entered this shop, I was immediately welcomed by the shop attendants and shown around the large collection of shoes on array. There were so many shoes within the shop, I thought within myself that if I had to try out all the shoes, it could take me several years to figure out which particular one to buy. I began to go from shelf to shelf, thinking which one to buy with the guidance of a shop attendant.

The attendant taking me round the shop was not helping my situation at all, he was trying his best to convince me on why I should buy each and every shoe. When we got to a new section of foot wears, he would immediately begin to list out all the characteristics and why that type of shoe was the best for me. The more the young man spoke, the more confused I became.

Eventually, I had gone through the shop for hours and had not spotted the right shoe for me. So I decided to do something about the situation or else my entire day was going to be spent at a shoe shop doing nothing. I proceeded to ask the attendant a few questions.

First I asked for a particular brand of shoe I had in mind. With enthusiasm, the young attendant led me to the part of the store where that shoe was. I promptly went about the particular shelf the guide showed me checking for the design that suited me. In no time, I had gotten the particular design that I wanted. My next task was to get my particular size which of course was the easiest thing to do. Within very few minutes I had gotten my particular size. I tried on the shoe with my design, with my size and with the colour I wanted and everything just matched perfectly fine. I was so proud I had gotten the best shoe for me. I moved few steps with it and it was perfect. I was elated and happy. Suddenly my eyes moved to the price tag on the shoes and that was when the unexpected happened, I stopped in my tracks.

"How can the shoes be this expensive" I asked the shop attendant with every surprise in my voice. I asked to buy a shoe, not a car, I told him".

We went to talk about the different prices of the shoes.

Though I had gotten the perfect shoe, with the perfect size, the perfect colour which suited me perfectly, none of this mattered when I saw the price tag that was on the shoe. Everything else suited me, except the price. The price did not suit me at all. In fact, on seeing the value of the shoe, I immediately dropped the pair and asked the young man to show me where cheaper shoes were sold. The shoe had a price which I could not afford.

My calm attendant then took me to another section of the store where I saw all manner of shoes. Like the section where the expensive shoes were, there were so many of them at the cheap section too. I walked about this section severally but could not find my type of shoe. But did that matter any longer? I had found what I loved but could not afford it, so now I had to go for what I could afford.

Without discrimination I immediately chose a shoe that was my size but did not look a bit like the design I needed. You may guess that it lacked the quality I desired too. But what could I do? I paid for my new cheap shoe and walked out of the shopping mall. Don't ask me if I was happy with what I got. Happy or not, I got what I could afford.

Why am I telling you this story? Because this life is particularly like that shoe store and all men are like the shoes within the shop.

Though the shop was called with a general term, A Shoe Store. Well, truth is, it never seemed that same way again when I got into the store. I learnt one golden rule of purchasing shoes. All shoes have value but shoes do not have same value.

Indeed within the shop, every shoe had a value but honestly different values. Though they were all called shoes, not all shoes were in same class. In fact, all the shoes were not put in same section.

While some shoes were made of the cheapest of leathers and rubber, some were made of the rarest of materials such as crocodile skins. While some shoes sold for a few dollars, there were some shoes in the store which sold for several hundreds of dollars. While some shoes were made by the manufacturer down the street, a few of the shoes were imported. And while some shoes were displayed loosely by the door, there were some too expensive that they were put in special show glasses.

What am I talking about? When you put together the material with which a shoe was made plus the cost of making it, together with where it was made, and the brand of the manufacture, you have what is called the net value or net worth of the shoe, hence its price also.

The price of a shoe like in my story determines who

and who cannot afford to purchase the shoe. You will also agree with me that who purchases the shoe determines how the shoe will be used. There are shoes so expensive you do not wear them every day.

I really do hope you get the point I am making. All men are like those shoes, we all have some worth but we do not have same net worth. As a matter of fact, we all have some value but our net value differs.

Have you noticed how at certain times in the news, you hear reports of several hundreds of people dying in a certain place at a time, yet their death changes nothing. However, there could be one man who when he dies alters the events that goes on around the world and puts the world to a standstill. I heard that the entire light in the world was put out the day the man who invented the light bulb, Thomas Edison died.

The difference between Thomas Edison and several of this other men who die without notice is in their net worth. Why the world remembers nothing of certain people, same world cannot forget some other people. The reason is the difference in the net worth they were able to build while on the earth.

Unlike the shoes which I used earlier in my illustration, every man from his worth can build and increase his net worth. You can build your net worth. You can build your net worth to rank in the likes of men such as Bill Gates, Steve Jobs, Mark Zuckerberg, and Warren Buffet of this world.

Irrespective of who you are, where you were born, what you can do or cannot do, irrespective of what your starting capital in life was, you can raise your value so high that you are needed for the most important jobs and invited for the most important meetings. You too can be a man of great net worth.

I am sure you have heard of the net worth of people being talked about. For example, in 2016 it was estimated that Bill Gates had a net worth of 78.7 billion dollars while his friend Warren Buffet was rated 74.2 billion dollars in net worth. Well, we may not like the idea or what is being done, but there is a grading system in this world that allows every man to be ranked. Whatever that grading system is, you do not have to be at the bottom of the ladder, you too can be among the best, among the most important, among the most valued, among the most influential. All you need to do is to learn the Secrets.

In this book, I have put together very vital principles and secrets that will help, in spite of where you are right now to increase your net worth many folds.

In fact, through this book, I have taught how you can estimate what you want your net worth to be and how you can practically move from where you are to where you want to be. No doubt you too will be a champion.

I hope that you do not just read this book but that you will digest every word. If you will go beyond reading this book to applying every principle that we have in the book, without any uncertainty, you too will rise to the apex of the ladder.

Come with me now and let me show you some timeless principles to increasing your net worth.

For the love of God, Church and Nation
Sunday Adelaja.

CHAPTER 1
....
YOU ALREADY HAVE
A WORTH

In this chapter, I am going to discuss critically about what I call your starting capital in life. You see every man has a starting capital in life and it is called worth, or self-worth. Your self-worth is totally different from your net worth. While you were born with a self-worth and is a gift of God to you to begin your life with, your net worth is what you build here on earth and what you choose to do with the resources and gifts that you have been given. The focus of this book is how to determine your net worth and how you create and increase net worth for yourself, however I must first remind you through this chapter that you have something already. You have a worth, a self-worth.

WHAT IS YOUR SELF-WORTH
AS A HUMAN BEING?

First of all we know we have worth because we are created in the image and the likeness of God. And we are people of worth because God lives in us. But that understanding that God lives in you might not be giving you any value. That understanding that God is in you might not be exploited and put to any use.

There a lot of people in life who though God lives and resides in them are still useless on the earth. So it is possible for God to live in a man and for that man to still be useless in life. A man though carrying God may be of no worth to himself, to his family, to his nation and to the people around him. God living in you will mean nothing to you, it might not be of any worth to you until you act on some things.

Through this book and beginning from this chapter, I am going to be focused on teaching you how to maximize the fact that you carry God, hence you have a worth. I am going to be focused on how you can convert that innate worth into your gross net worth on the earth. You can accomplish, you can be a champion, you can dominate, and you can reign on earth with the virtue of your net worth.

NO MAN WAS BORN EMPTY

No man was born empty, every man was born with a worth. It is only left for you to leverage on that worth and convert your worth into your net worth.

For example, I once had an experience which can be used for the perfect illustration. I was in Singapore at a time. While I was there I had some pastors from America with me who were pastors of Nigerian descent. They wanted to travel with me and I obliged them. There were other Pastors with me also; some Swedish pastors, some Russian pastors and some Native American pastors with me.

What I noticed was that each time I wanted to do anything, the Nigerian pastors would run to me and always tried to help me.

One particular day, we were going to the airport. My main bags were in the hand of my assistant but I had two little bags with me which were just handbags. One of the Nigerian pastors came to me to help me with the handbags. This young man already had two heavy bags with him, yet he started dragging my two small bags from me, wanting to take the bags from me. He said to me 'You are our Apostle, you should not be carrying anything'

When I saw that he was not going to give up easily, I replied him and I said, *"If you didn't have anything in your hands already, perhaps I would oblige you. You are already carrying too much. It will be wrong for me to allow you carry so much burden while I do nothing with my hands. Why should you be taking mine as well?"*

He insisted on helping me and when I saw I was not going to win with him, I gave him one of the bags.

The other pastor of African descent came also and wanted to take the other little thing in my hand. I was embarrassed. Now this scene at the airport was disturbing enough, what was more disturbing was the fact that there were ladies that were carrying their bags to the airport as well and nobody was trying to help them. Many of the ladies were on same trip as us and many of them were struggling so much under the weight of their burden, yet none of the young men offered to help them.

When these two Pastors took my bags from me, I went immediately to carry the bags from the ladies and I carried the bags for the ladies.

Just as I did that, my dear young Pastors came again to me and started dragging the ladies' bags from me. In addition to the many bags they already had, they would want to do anything to ensure I was not carrying any bag, whereas they cared less that the ladies were carrying as much or much more.

When I realised what was happening, I knew these young men needed to be schooled. I called them and began speaking to them, I said *"I understand that you want to honour me, I appreciate you for that. However, when your hands are busy and my hands are not as busy as yours, then you should let me carry my bags. If you have two hands with which you are already carrying things, I have two hands also and my hands can still work. I'm not invalid, I'm not paralyzed, I'm not incapacitated just allow me to use my hands"*.

I went on to tell them that because they were all over me, that was why I succumbed and allowed them.

They appreciated me for talking to them on those things. However, I would not let them go until I gave them the more important lesson. I told these my dear friends how I noticed that they were so concerned about carrying my bags. Yet, there were ladies who were carrying heavier bags than me and they cared less. They were not paying any attention to them, they were not even thinking about helping the ladies. So it was only when I took the bags from the women that they ran to me.

While the ladies were carrying such heavy bags, none of them offered to help the ladies, none of them offered to take the bags from those ladies. Now, when I took the bags from the women, that was when they rushed to me, wanting to carry the bags and take the bags from me again.

That gave me so much concern, it revealed a lot about their mind-set. It revealed how much value we place on people. It showed that we fail to often realise that every man has an innate worth. What makes a man worthy and that which gives him worth is not title and status, it is the mere fact that he is a human being, created in God's own image. A lot of minds have been so brainwashed.

Still speaking to these my dear young friends I said, *"Why do you think you have to carry my bags and not those of the women? First of all I have my hands and I could use my hands, you needed not bother yourselves even because your hands are already busy. If I have hands, they are meant to be used.*

Secondly, even if you want to help anybody and you are so generous, if you are so kind that you want to help people, then there are real needs around us here. The real needs are with the women. First reason being that they are women, they are weaker vessels and should not be allowed to carry heavy loads." The fact that the young pastors didn't know that broke my heart. I told them to go help the women. I told them to go help anyone who genuinely needs their help. The women needed help more than I did. They are the ones who needed their bags to be carried, their struggle and pain was begging for help more than I was begging for help, In fact I didn't need their help.

DO YOU SEE THE WORTH IN OTHERS?

It is unfortunate that many people today cannot realise the need around them. They cannot sense the worth in people. They cannot listen and hear the cry and groans of people around them. They cannot help others realise their self-worth. They do not appreciate the value that every man possesses.

Again, let me emphasise to you that every man that

you see upon the earth has some value within him already. Hence you should treat every man you come across on the earth with that worth and appreciation.

Yes, it does not matter who they are. It does not matter what title or titles go before their first name. It does not matter what schools they have been to, how many degrees they have or whether they have no degree at all. What is most important is that they are human beings and they already have a great measure of worth.

Whose needs do you notice? Who do you observe as being in need? Whose cries catch your attention? Who do you see as needy even though they are not expressing their need with any word?

You have to understand and appreciate the value in people before you can notice those in need and be of help. If not you will be pouring your water into the ocean, you will be offering assistance where it is not needed. You will be wasting your time and your worth.

That is what I see happening all over the world today. People will only commend and give words of affirmation to the CEO (Chief Executive Officer) who gets affirmation from a lot of people already rather than the janitor whose very essence is crying out for it.

People will rather appreciate a man who wears one suit out of the several he has got and refuse to validate the man who has put the only suit he has into shape and has worn it on his back. People will rather pass by the weak, the lame, the beggars, the orphans, the tormented, the widows and take their large offerings to church, to the man of God who already has mansions and jets. What shallow mindedness.

The point I am trying to establish and to help you

see is that every man has a worth. Every man is worthy. Oprah Winfrey, the renowned television lady and talk-show host in the United States once shared something remarkable. She said in almost her thirty years of hosting the talk-show, and it does not matter who was invited, once the cameras are down, every single one of her guests over the years turned to her to ask *'How was it?'*, *'How did I perform'? 'Tell me it was okay'*. Every one asked same questions, from the President of the United states to the lowly housewife who was invited to share her story. Everyone asked same questions.

Basically, what she was saying is that every human being on earth is the same and our very being is crying out for same needs. Every man wants commendation, so do not just commend your boss, commend those who are under you. Every man wants to be appreciated, so do not just commend your secretary, commend your wife at home too. Every man wants love, love all men.

In Nigeria for example, we have a lot of poor people who are daily labouring and languishing, many of them are hoping for any help. The statistics of people living in abject poverty in Nigeria is almost 65%, which is more than 100 million people in total. How come these people are not being helped? How come we do not see any of these people to give assistance to, we would rather give assistance to only people who can help us in return. That is selfishness and not true help.

How come you do not notice people?

How come you do not notice people? How come you do not even notice the crying and the hurting? How come you are not even paying attention to them?

If you want to help anybody, go help people in need. I am not in need, why is everyone rushing to help me? sometimes is the question I ask myself.

In the story I shared earlier, I told the Pastors that those same women they did not help have same innate worth as I do, yet they failed to help them. As soon as I went to help the women however, the Pastors came rushing to me, not to the ladies, but to me to take their bags from me. It shows the level of their mind and the state of understanding that they have got.

One of the Pastors that I was challenging was the boldest, he was the senior pastor of his own ministry. He immediately came to their defence. I asked him to explain to me if there was something I was missing. He told me that they are only honouring my position. They are only honouring my title. They only pay honour because I was their mentor and Pastor Sunday.

So I asked them what my position was. What is it to honour in a name or in a title? I can't remember the exact answer I was given but one of them said they needed to serve the anointing.

According to them, I was the one who was the anointed one. I was the big person among them, I was the pastor and because of that they had to serve me.

In my estimate, such a thought is one of the mothers of all evil in the world today. It is what makes a man place value on one life and destroy the next life. It is such a thought that gives education to some children and denies millions and billions of other children access to good education. It is what gives opulence to certain people while others can die in penury. It is what makes a household eat as much as they want to for dinner, throw everything else away while many other households cannot eat a meal, three days in a row. Such a thought is anti-God, it is against the Kingdom of God.

If you cannot treat everyone with same respect as you give to your pastor, then you are a fake person. That is also eye-service. You are only massaging the ego of somebody and do not truly respect them. True respect respects all men, it values all people.

I told the young men that day not to tell me that they were deciding my worth based on what I have done, based on my achievements or reputation. Unfortunately, that is what the world does. The world seems to have certain criteria with which it judges the value of people. The world judges people by money and status in the society, educational achievements, even racial background. This is unfortunate.

Continuing in my discussion with the Pastors in Singapore, I told them it was good to honour the anointing, even the Bible told us to honour our men of God, but I wanted to know if they knew the reason why I went to get the bags from the women. So turning to the one who was next to me, I asked him *"why did I your apostle go to the ladies to collect their bags?"*

He took a minute to think, then he mumbled some words. I wanted him to be clear so I told him to speak up. He said he thinks I probably wanted to help them because they are women.

His response got me laughing. What got me laughing was something missing in his answer. So I said to him "okay but you also saw them as women, why didn't you help them because they are women?'

I had not landed when one of them said again, *"Pastor Sunday, but you are the pastor, you are the man of God."*

So I pulled their attention closely and taught them some clear principles. At the end of our discussion, I said to them,

"If you really want to follow me and be my disciple, if you want me to be your mentor and you want to be my mentee, then you need to understand my philosophy".

What is my philosophy? Let me tell you my philosophy, my philosophy is that everyone deserves to be honoured, every human being has a worth.

WHY MUST A MAN BE HONOURED?

What makes a man deserving of honour? Why must a man be honoured? The answer is not far-fetched, because he is a human being. You only need to be a human being to be honoured. Every human being on earth has God's nature within them. Every human being on earth has worth. Everybody has worth not because of what they've achieved. Everybody has worth because of who they are and whose they are.

For the secular world, they view your worth by what you have done and achieved. That is worldly. That is the way they see it and it is worldly thinking.

For those with a higher mind-set, for Christians and those who want to live the right way, we should see and treat people differently. We should give everybody honour, we should give everybody worth because they are made in the image and likeness of God. Every human deserves to be respected, every human deserves to be honoured.

Now, those women in my story deserved to be given

double honour. First, because they are human beings and secondly because they are women, they are the weaker vessels. That's just logical, a woman has to be loved and shown affection. Women do not have the strength that men have. That is just sensible, you don't need to be a Christian to be kind and nice to the ladies. As a man, women shouldn't be carrying heavy bags around you and you are looking on, you are the stronger one, you have the stronger body mass and frame, use that to help people.

Now earlier and through the thoughts that I shared, everyone has a need for honour, affirmation and validation. Everyone has a need for help. It is the silent noise that goes around with everybody and does not leave them. There are 7 billion people in the world today and every one of us has need for one form of help or the other.

Everyone needs something. So when you meet a man next, pay attention to that which is about him that is crying out for help. He could be dressed in expensive suits, exuding sweet smell from his strong cologne, do not be deceived, that man has a need. As long as he is human he has a need. Every one of us has a need. The Pastor has a need as much as the gardener of the church. The waiter has a need as much as the man who owns the restaurant.

Everybody that has need must be helped, it doesn't have to be just the pastor. I told the Pastors at the airport in Singapore, that though I was their Pastor and mentor, if there was ever a situation where they needed help, I would help them. If the ladies were not there with bags, struggling to carry load, and I happen to meet them as young men at the airport with their hands full, I would help them. If my hands were free, I will not just pass by them. I will immediately rush to them to help them with their loads and bag, though I was their leader, teacher and mentor.

I told my Pastors, *"I will not allow you to carry all the loads by yourself. If the ladies were not here and your hands were full, I Pastor Sunday will be carrying your bags."*

Those Pastors laughed and immediately objected, they said, *"No pastor, we will not allow that. We cannot allow you to carry our bags."*

Now if you know me and if you know those around me, what I said to these Pastors is what you already know too well. I carry bags for my members, I open doors for them, I hold their seat for them, I do all of these because it's logical. That as far as I am concerned is the sensible thing to do. I do not do any of those things because I am a Christian nor is it because I am Pastor, rather because I am just logical and sensible. That is what I call basic human behaviour. This is what you ought to know and do before we can call you a human being at all.

I have two hands, you also have two hands. Your two hands are busy, my two hands are free. It's just common sense that I should come and help you because my hands are free. But those my Pastor friends were saying they would not allow me to do that because I'm a pastor. I was ashamed because I knew they were Pastors too, what they were inadvertently saying was that they would never do that for their own members.

Your Position does not
determine your worth

It is not your position that decides your worth, it is not your achievement that determines your worth. What decides your worth is that you are human. Just the fact that you are human itself gives you worth. It also makes you to be deserving of worth, honour and respect.

So it's just pure logic that I see that you are over-loaded and that I should help you. I just have to be human. It shows I am human.

"Oh pastor you are the big man". You are a big man too because God lives in you. It's not just pastors that deserve to be honoured. The bible says give honour to whom honour is due. While it is okay to honour your pastor, to honour people in higher position, it is what the general people do. It is what is common, no one needs to be taught to do that.

However, more importantly than those people in higher position, we must honour people who are lower than us. Real men treat the gateman with same respect as the Chairman.

Again, on what basis must you do that, because the bible says that we should honour all men. Honour all men, even pastors must honour their members and those in higher positions should honour those who are in lower positions.

It's a tragedy the kind of churches, sanctuaries, companies and organizations we have today. We make the members not just to honour the pastor but to worship them. It's only the members honouring and adoring the pastors. It is only the employees who honour the employer, it is never the other way round.

Not only do we allow those who are below us honour us, respect us and almost worship us, many times we treat these people like they are our property. We dehumanise them, we rob them of their dignity and pride. We task people on what we cannot do ourselves or tasks we cannot allow any of our loved ones to do.

If you are a boss at work reading this, I charge you to honour those who work for you. If you are a housewife who has come in contact with this book, I challenge you to give honour to the maids and young girls in your home working for you. If you are a husband reading this, I challenge you to take out time to honour your wife and go out of your way to do the unusual for her. This must not be a one-time event. You must do this every day and consistently till it becomes your new life style.

Many pastors and chief executives think they are the only ones who deserve to receive the honour. But that is wrong, a pastor is supposed to give honour to his members as well. A chief executive is supposed to give honour to people on his payroll same way that those people honour him. We all are meant to honour all men because God is in everyman.

YOU HONOUR GOD WHEN
YOU HONOUR ALL MEN

You see my friend, you cannot truly honour God if you cannot honour all men. You can only honour God when you honour men. You only honour God to the extent to which you honour men. You cannot truly honour God that you cannot see if you cannot honour the men that you see here all the time. So you cannot truly honour God if all you do is dishonour men.

I have seen men who will mistreat their wives and immediately jump into the car, on their way to a worship service. I have seen a lot of women who disregard their husbands and make life for such men miserable, yet these women honour their Pastors so much, the one who does not live with them at home. So many women will rain abuses and curses on their own husbands, yet cannot look the Pastor or their boss at work in the eye.

When you practise such selective honour, you are only destroying yourself, you are not honouring God. We tend to look down on what is around us and term it as common. We tend to only honour only the people we think we will need help from. You are not to just honour those who can help you, you are to also honour those who are so weak that they cannot render help to you.

In the Scriptures, Jesus said I was naked, and you did nothing about it. When you saw the poor guy and you looked down on him, it was not the poor guy that was naked, Jesus said he was the one that was naked.

Back to that same scriptural reference, why did the people immediately respond like that? Why did they say that they didn't see Jesus naked? They didn't see him naked because they were not looking for the poor guy, they were not looking for the ordinary people. They were looking for Jesus. They were looking for the guy with the shiny face and clothes of fire. We look for the supernatural, and despise the ordinary things. Yet, God is often in the ordinary things, that is why it is so easy to miss Him.

Now Jesus gave them a shocker, Jesus said that the way you treat every ordinary person that is naked, that is hungry, that is sick, the way you attend to the beggars, the blind, the weak, is the way you are treating me. As a teacher at school, the way you treat your students, as a doctor and nurse, the way you treat your patients, as a banker and office-person, the way you treat your clients, as a prison warden, the way you treat the prisoners, that's the same way you are treating God.

Jesus was very emphatic when he said, it's me, that's me that you were attending to. I was the one you neglected, I was the one you bypassed, I was the one you didn't honour, I was the one you didn't respect, I was the one you spat on, I was the one you hissed at. Yes I was the one. I was the orphan child around your house with torn clothes. I was the widow whose situation you knew about and you did nothing. I was the child at school whose tuition could not be paid and got thrown out of school. That was me and that is me.

So Jesus didn't say it was the poor man you didn't feed, he said you didn't feed him. He didn't say it was the poor man that was hungry, Jesus was the one that was hungry. So it's not about you and the poor man, it's not about you and the hungry or wretched man, it's about you and God. That is how God sees it.

Is it not incredible how we tend to overlook people and we claim to serve God. It is incredible how we can jump over people in need and run to be part of a worship service, thinking we are serving God that way. Is it not amazing how we overlook the potholes, the death traps on the very roads that lead to our cathedrals? We wouldn't serve people, but we claim to be serving God. Again, what a tragedy.

So I personally think that if you go to a church where they only teach you how to honour the pastors, the big men and the church leaders, you are supposed to be on your way out of such a citadel, in fact run away from that church.

God does not look at people same way that man looks at people. Far from it. God measures us differently.

"A great man is going to die"

Many years ago I read the story of a particular Church. It was a very interesting story and it will help you understand what I am discussing with you better. In that story, God revealed to this church that he was going to take someone special to Him away from them. It was told them that a great and significant man in their midst was going to die.

The church immediately began to fast and pray, not wanting to lose any great man in their midst. It so happened that all the emphasis of their prayers was for their Pastors and deacons. They would mention the name of each Pastor and deacon and the large donors in their church to God in prayer. Everyone began to do all that they could do to pray for those they considered 'great' and 'significant' among them.

Two weeks later, the Church gardener died and people hardly noticed. Nobody cried or mourned, they were too busy praying against the death of their Pastors and the significant people in Church. Several months later, the whole Church was still busy praying and fasting.

Eventually, God spoke again to the Church that the one dear to his heart, the great and significant person had long been taken. There was no need for such prayers again. So while the whole church was so focused on their

Pastors and the large donors, to God the great man was the church gardener. Lessons learnt.

Everybody deserves honour, everybody deserves to be respected, and everybody is valuable. What makes you valuable is not the money you have, it is not the position you occupy. Of course those things are important, they make you valuable too.

The fundamental value and worth that you have is first of all the fact that God is in you. You are made and created in the image of God. That is the most important thing that makes you valuable first of all.

You are God's likeness and the bible tells us that if you don't love your neighbour that is nearby, then you cannot truly love God. There is no way you can claim to love God if you don't love people. And we can only love people when we value them.

HIGHLIGHTS
FROM CHAPTER ONE

1. Every man has a starting capital in life and it is called worth, or self-worth.

2. Your self-worth is totally different from your net worth.

3. There are a lot of people in life who though God lives and resides in them are still useless on the earth.

4. A man though carrying God may be of no worth to himself, to his family, to his nation and to the people around him.

5. Every man that you see upon the earth has some value within him already. Hence you should treat every man you come across on the earth with worth and appreciation.

6. My philosophy is that everyone deserves to be honoured. Every human being must be honoured.

7. Everyone needs something. Every man has a need.

CHAPTER 2

....

RESPONDING TO THE WORTH WITHIN YOU

In the first chapter, we have looked critically at the fact that every man has a worth within him. We have also discussed why it is very paramount and essential for you to respond appropriately to the worth that each man possesses.

Again, I must remind you that beyond having a worth, there is that which is called a net worth and that is what I will focus on in this entire book. Earlier in the book, I explained to you that every man has a worth but not every man has a net worth. We will consider these matters in greater details later in the book. Having discussed extensively on the worth which every man possesses and how we should respond to that, we will shortly consider and talk about net worth. I will explain to you the issues concerning your net worth, I want to help you define your net worth.

YOU HAVE A WORTH

The whole aim of this entire book is helping you to build, create and increase your net worth. I am going to delve into that shortly but before I do that, it is very appropriate that I teach you how to respond to your own worth. Some people understand the worth in others but fail to acknowledge the worth in themselves. Before we can consider strategies in building your net worth, the foundation is for you to understand your own worth and how to respond in the right ways to the worth that you carry and possess.

I have taught you that every man has a worth and I have taught you how to respond to the worth in people. However, you have a worth too and I must teach you how to respond to your own worth. Without your worth, there can be no net worth. Unless you appreciate who you are, what you have and what you can do with what you have, there will never be anything like the creation of net worth, building of net worth, building of value etcetera.

If there is any foundation that has to be laid and solidified first of all, it has to be the value of knowing your worth and what demands you can make based on that worth.

So right now, we are discussing about your worth. What is your worth and what implications does it have for you? Later on, we will shift our focus to how you can convert your worth into your net worth.

I'm laying the base and under-structure about your worth before I get into your net worth. Building your net worth is one of the most important topics you will ever learn in life, however before you can learn how to build your net worth it is crucial and important that you learn what your worth is and what implications it has for your life and destiny.

We have picked our discussions carefully in a way that the real essence of the book will not be lost, that is building your net worth.

YOUR WORTH IS WHAT
YOU HAVE GOT IN YOU

You are a child of God, you are the image of God. Even though we honour all men, we honour Presidents and Governors, we honour Kings and queens, we honour Prime Ministers, pastors and ministers. Though it is good to honour all these people, I'm not saying you should not honour them or disregard them. However, the very important thing is that you also deserve to be honoured.

I do not know who you are right now and I do not know what state of life that you are in. However, one thing is true, certain and definite, you deserve to be honoured. You must be honoured. You have a worth, you have dignity, you are a person of distinction, you are privileged, there is God's glory upon you, you've got your own prestige and fame, you have merit, credit, and importance, you are of an illustrious birth and heritage, you are notable.

Kings, queens, presidents and their allies, pastors and all people too must honour you. You know already that in life Parents too must honour their children. If a parent only demands that his children should honour him and he won't honour the children in return, then those children are going to become rebellious one way or the other. Either such a father or mother likes it or not, those children will walk away and far from him or her.

In same manner, if there is an organisation or system that only puts people into slavery, if there is any system, church or organization that only subjects people and forces everyone to bow down to just one man, then that system is breeding chaos. It is like the adage of sitting on a keg powder or a time bomb, it will detonate sooner than later.

LET NO MAN ENSLAVE YOU

Let no one enslave you, let no one put you in a bondage, do not allow any man bend you before himself. By the way nobody should bow down to another man. Nobody should worship another man. There is no scriptural basis for that and that is what Jesus was trying to teach us. It was also what he was trying to correct when he said don't call anybody father, don't call anybody teacher.

It's not that you should not call anybody father or teacher as a title, you can use the words father or teacher for a man. The main idea though that Jesus was trying to teach and to pass across was that we must not elevate people to the point of worshipping them. Don't elevate people so much as to degrading your own value or your own worth. Don't elevate people so much that you see yourself as nothing.

My dear friend, what is your name? Paul, Richard, Jane, whatever your name is, I plead with you friend, don't ever be in a system or a church where they make you feel as if you are nothing.

Such a system may offer you a few things as benefits but what they are taking away from you is what can never be replaced. What is being stolen is your dignity, it is your worth and it is your capability. What is being robbed from you is the very essence of your soul. Do not give any man on earth the right to reduce you to the shadows of a human being.

Don't ever remain in a system where they pull down your worth, your honour, your glory. That should never happen. Do not give any man that right, in spite of whatever name he bears or title he carries. Whether it's pastor, apostle, bishop, doctor or your boss at work, nobody has the right to humiliate you or dishonour you. Don't allow men to dehumanize you.

DO NOT BE TRAINED WITH THE ELEMENT OF DISGRACE

Don't allow men to use disgrace as a method of training you. Don't allow people to shame or to break you. We should never use shame to teach people. We should never use disgrace to say *"I'm just teaching you a lesson"*.

Don't ever use disgrace to teach people. When you use shame, disgrace, dishonour, disrespect as a way of teaching somebody, you destroy their humanity, you disgrace their humanity and you shatter their humanity. You bring down the honour of God that is upon their lives. The bible says that God has crowned us with glory and honour. Psalms 8:5 says **"You have made them a little lower than the angels and crowned them with glory and honour"**

The goal of the slave master is to break the spirit of the slaves, the goal of the oppressor is to destroy and shatter your spirit. The goal of torture is to make you hopeless and to make you see why you can never do anything in life without them. When you are under such systems, you are really under manipulative systems, that is control, that is witchcraft. You have got to run for your life. You understand now why it is important for every man to first build his worth before we can ever have the mention of building net worth.

Listen to me my friend, God is saying to you, don't you allow any human being to dishonour you, to disgrace you, to disrespect you. No matter what you have done or what has happened. No matter what your past or background is, no matter what grounds anybody has against you. Do not allow men to debase you.

Even if anyone is going to discipline you, then let them discipline you out of love. Even if they are going to punish you, let them punish you out of love. But they should not touch your glory, they should not touch your honour, they should not touch your worth.

You should never allow any human on earth to pull down your worth, your humanity. The bible says God the creator of heaven and earth so much honours you. Can you imagine that, God honours you and me?

EVEN GOD DOES NOT SHAME YOU, WHY SHOULD A MAN?

God honours us so much that even God will not disgrace you in any way. Even God will not dishonour you. Why will God not disgrace you? Because if He dishonours you, He dishonours Himself. Hence any man who dishonours you dishonours God.

God will not dishonour a man because it will mean he will be going against Himself. God would rather put honour upon your head. God is an elevator of your head, He is the lifter of your head. He doesn't put shame on you. He doesn't pull you down, He doesn't disgrace you. He will not humiliate you. God rather gives you honour. He crowns you, there is a crown of honour on your head.

There is a crown of glory on your head, don't let any human being remove that glory, that honour, that importance. It's not just the pastor that is crowned with glory and honour, it's not just ministers who are crowned with glory and honour, every one of us is crowned with glory and honour.

Somebody said don't touch me because I am anointed and do me no harm because I am a prophet. You are anointed too so don't let anybody touch your anointing. You are also the apple of God's eye. We are all made in God's image.

By the way, anybody that pulls a fellow human being down, anybody that humiliates another person, the person who humiliates is humiliating God. God said that if you humiliate the poor, you are humiliating not just the poor, but also his creator. It's not just the needy and the weak, if you humiliate anybody, if you mistreat any human being, you are mistreating his creator.

I have heard different horrible stories of how people who are highly placed, people who should use their authority and strength to defend the weak use same authorities to demean the people. I have heard this also, I don't know if it's true that some pastors slap their church members. Some even slap their assistant pastors, maybe not physical slaps but many shout at people publicly and from open stage. Such act is called public shaming. If it is not done with the intention of bringing people's value down, then it is evil. No man should disgrace another man. I want to believe people do that because they are ignorant.

YOU BELONG TO THE BEST PLACES IN LIFE

The scriptures enjoins us not to have reserved places

for pastors or anybody, not to become hypocritical and engage in the acts of the Pharisees and Sadducees. But today's churches are reserving places as if they don't read the Bible. When you see the 'thrones' of some men of God, you might really get confused as to who sits on those thrones, whether men or God.

Unfortunately, a lot of these things are happening in our churches today. In the church where I pastor and indeed all of our Churches, we have the first row where the Pastors sit. But those seats are common and same as those everyone else sit on. We do this because everyman has value and must be treated properly. There is no seat set up that you must not be able to sit on in life. The best places are for you too.

During our Church services, people go on to the stage to dance or for one thing or the other, when they are done some of them choose to remain in the front row and sit around me and every other person.

This often is alarming for some pastors who visit us from different parts of the world. After services, some of them come to me to ask, *"Pastor, what was that. Why will you just allow anyone sit with you."*

After the message and I make altar calls, some of these people who come forward are those who want to give their life to Christ. It is at such moments these guest pastors know and realise that some of these people are not even born again.

In fact, in a particular scenario, one of the newly converted persons took my seat and I sat in the next place to him. My guests often wouldn't believe that was happening. They couldn't believe what their eyes saw.

That is because we have elevated ourselves above any

other human. This shouldn't be. In fact as a matter of fact if you are anointed, God has elevated you, and it is to serve other people. If you have been anointed by God, you are to serve other people. If you want to be the first, you have to be willing to want to be a slave, you have to be willing to be the last. If you want to be the greatest, you have to be willing to be the least. That is just the way this kingdom works.

WHAT MAKES YOU HAVE WORTH?

All of us have worth not just because of the positions we have or because of the money we have, or because we are pastors or not. We have worth because God created us. He created us in his image.

You don't even have to be a Christian to have worth. It is not just Christians who have worth, unbelievers have worth because they are created in God's image. Christians have worth because they are created in God's image. Muslims have worth. There are at least one billion Hindus in the world today and each of them has a worth too. Every human being is supposed to be equally respected because they are created in God's image and likeness.

We are supposed to exalt people, to honour people. We are not supposed to disgrace people, not to humiliate, not to break people. In same manner, you must not allow or permit anyone treat you lesser than you deserve.

You are supposed to love people, to bless them and to show them the love of Christ and it must be vice versa. I am not saying you are to live your life expecting these things from people, but I am saying that you do not hang around people who will treat you otherwise.

I love to continue with my earlier example, if God honours people and he says don't give a special place to people in the church, we shouldn't do it. It means don't have preferential treatment in the church. Too sad, some people are doing exactly that. We shouldn't do that, we should be like our father who is in heaven. We should honour people.

The special seat is a symbol of the fact that we are not to put some people above other people. Make sure that everybody is treated equally. That is the way things are in the kingdom of God. We should know that everybody deserves honour, everybody deserves respect, not because of who they are or what they have but because God's image is in them, God lives in them. Even if they are not born again or our church folks, God's image is in them still, so we have to honour them.

(I will have to say here however, that the special seats are made for order, in that case, it is understandable but order must not be a reason for putting down the dignity of another)

SPECIAL WORD FOR WOMEN AND WIVES

Permit me at this point in our discussion to address women and wives. Often times in talking about oppression and being disrespected, women are the worst hit.

I'm sure discussing issues of women is fast becoming sensitive issues, I know I'm going to a dangerous place now but it is imperative for me to still talk about it. So if you are a woman and you are reading this, then read carefully.

My advice to women and wives is not to allow any silly man anywhere beat and pound them and they still remain in that house. Don't allow anybody to humiliate or to constantly embarrass, mortify and shame the nature of God in you to that extent.

Abuse is not just the physical torture you receive. There are many other forms of abuse and varied ways by which abuse is being done and carried out. Don't allow moral abuse. Don't allow anybody to denigrate you and put you down. You have been crowned with glory by your father.

The bible says that men must treat women as co-heirs of God's inheritance. Men must treat women as princesses. I call my wife "Princess" because the bible says I must treat her as the daughter of the most high God.

Women must be treated with honour. The bible says husbands must treat their wives with love and honour. They are daughters of the king. Don't allow anybody to emotionally abuse you, mentally abuse you or sexually abuse you. Don't allow anybody to humiliate you.

If anybody tries it, call the police or law enforcement agents on him and get him to the prison, that's the rightful place for such a man.

If the police will not come to get him, take your bags, pack your materials and with confidence tell him *"just to let you know that you will never see me here again. If you are a brute, go and be a brute to another animal, you can't be a brute to me. Go and be a brute to wild animals, go and be a brute to whoever you want. One thing is certain, you can't be a brute to me"*

Let everyone know who you are. Raise your shoulders high and your head straight. Tell anyone who cares to listen to who you are *"I'm a daughter of the almighty God. I will not allow any man to remove the glory that God has put on me. I will not allow any human to reduce my glory, to reduce my honour. I will not allow any human to humiliate me, I will not allow anyone to put me lower than where God has placed me"*

Read again carefully, I'm not saying you should go and divorce, I'm just saying pack your load and leave that place.

Someone might probably be telling you to endure. People may say that through your endurance, God is going to save the brute through you.

Attention! Let God save the person Himself. You are not the Saviour of the world, it is God who is the Saviour of the world. It is God who created him, God knows how to save him. Let God save him by Himself. You are not going to save him. You are not the rescuer and the liberator of the world, you didn't die for him. Let God save him without your help. God has millions of people in this world, He has millions of ways that He can use to save him.

DON'T DIE FOOLISHLY IN THE
HAND OF THE OPPRESSOR

Don't talk yourself into enduring humiliation, don't endure unnecessary abuse just because you are thinking God will use you to save the abuser. Don't die cheaply. Do not wait until your oppressor kills you.

Dying in that manner is just foolishness, it's just stupidity. Don't wait till anyone kills you. Save yourself before someone will have to come and save you. Get that kind of brute out of your life. Don't allow anybody to abuse you.

Same thing goes with men. It is not only women who

suffer abuse. As a matter of fact, I read a very interesting article the other day which claims men tend to be more victims of abuse than women, simply because they are too ashamed to talk about it, and when they do, no one will believe them.

We all have the honour and glory of God upon us. Don't allow anybody to humiliate that glory, to despise that God that is in you. Let the honour of God that is in you be seen. Let your worth be seen. That is how to acknowledge the worth that you possess and carry within you.

I have seen on the Internet over the years certain strange things that people do. I see how religion is killing people in Africa. I see how Churches which should elevate people have become centres for debasing people. I see also strange things that pastors in African churches do. In Southern part of the continent especially, it is extremely difficult for me to understand some of the things I have seen like church members eating grasses. I read also that a woman was killed because the Pastor put a very large box of speaker on her chest.

Someone needs to start a campaign against all these things, maybe that's someone's calling. I once saw a pastor in Africa stepping on a woman's pregnant stomach. All in the name of miracle. Don't let anyone just do anything to you in the name of miracle. Don't allow anybody to humiliate you.

You have worth because of what God has done for you, you have worth because of the God that lives in you. You have worth and you deserve to be honoured and respected.

Now that you understand your worth, now that you

know that when it comes to worth, no one is superior to you in life. Now that you understand that there is nothing any man has in life that you do not have a right to. How do you build your net worth? That will be our focus from the next chapter.

HIGHLIGHTS
FROM CHAPTER TWO

1. Some people understand the worth in others but fail to acknowledge the worth in themselves.

2. Unless you appreciate who you are, what you have and what you can do with what you have, there will never be anything like the creation of net worth

3. Building your net worth is one of the most important topics you will ever learn in life

4. You must be honoured. You have a worth, you have dignity, you are a person of distinction, you are privileged, there is God's glory upon you.

5. We have worth because God created us. He created us in his image.

6. Don't talk yourself into enduring humiliation, don't endure unnecessary abuse just because you are thinking God will use you to save the abuser.

7. Let your worth be seen. That is how to acknowledge the worth that you possess and carry within you.

CHAPTER 3
....

IDENTIFYING YOUR
NET WORTH

Having understood the power of your personal worth, we can now proceed to discuss how to build your net worth.

Your net worth is the sum total of your relevance to your environment and to your world. Your net worth is defined by how many people have need of you and what problems you are actually solving. Your net worth is determined by your applicability on the earth. How applicable are you? What is your importance? What is your purpose? What are we missing if you are not around? What would this world have missed if you were not born? Answers to all of these are what actually determine your net worth on the earth.

Again I must emphasize that you must not confuse your worth with your net worth. While every man was born with a worth, not every man has a net worth. Net worth is built. It is the choices that you make that determines your net worth and the products and value that comes out of you.

In this chapter, I am going to teach you how you can create your net worth, using every tangible and intangible material that you have got around you.

WHY I DO NOT DRIVE, WHY MY WIFE DOES NOT COOK

Some years ago, I preached a sermon to a group of people. I spoke to the people on why I do not drive and why my wife does not cook. The essence of the whole sermon was to help people create their net worth and see how time is the essence of life. It was a nice sermon and I must say I had a great time with the people, or so I thought until the responses to my message began to pour in. I could not believe what the responses of the people were to my sermon.

I received a lot of unpleasant responses from people. Even though everything I said in the message was true. Over the years, I have created the culture of one thing and that is the culture of saying the truth.

I could say things you don't like but what I say is always true. Nothing can be done against the truth but for the truth. If you do not agree or you do agree, the bottom line is everything I said is what I mean and it is true.

Even though that message was titled 'Why my wife does not cook and I do not drive' the point in that message was different. The point that I was passing across is not to encourage women not to cook or for men not to drive as many of the people who wrote to me afterwards assumed. That was not the main thing I wanted to communicate to the people.

I thought the people understood that it was an illustration I gave to them. It was an example and illustration and was not a commandment or decree. I was not saying everyone should be like that or operate their lives like that. I would have preferred for it to be so or for everyone to be like that. It was just a sharing of experience and a recommendation for men to do same.

I understand that not everyone has that possibility. My wife too fought the idea initially for almost three years, I had to convince her on the point I was making.

Now what is the essence of the message and what point was I bringing across? That is the whole essence of this book. It is about a subject which is one of the most important issues to your existence on earth. If you will be relevant on this side of eternity, if your life will have any use, if you will be a person of caliber and value, then you must understand this subject I am talking about. The subject is called net worth and how to increase your net worth.

If you will pay careful attention to this truth, it will change your life and transform you. A careful acknowledgement of this truth will give you more results in a few years than you have ever gotten in your entire life. How do I know that?

First, I must tell you why my wife does not cook and I do not drive. Why did I make this decision many years ago?

IT'S NOT ABOUT COOKING AND DRIVING, IT'S ABOUT THIS VALUE

I made this decision because of something I already understood. That is the way I treat my wife and women generally. I've been asked often by people who cannot afford such a life, many have expressed concerns like my wife expressed initially, *'What if I cannot afford a cook for my wife?'* When people ask me such questions, I realize they have not come to the full understanding of what I am about to tell you. They are still stuck in the illustration of the message.

Many years ago, I spoke with my wife on this pertinent issue. My goal was to help her see the need in creating self-worth. I said to her

"Princess, I have worked very hard all my life to get to this point when I can afford anything for you. I have built my life to come to a place when nothing will be too costly or too expensive for me to do for you. I prepared myself and worked hard. Now that I have attained this, I need you to stop cooking for me or for the children or our entire family all together."

My wife may cook for leisure, but she will never cook because she has to do it. I ensured that.

You see, I did not get to that stage in one day. However, the fundamental understanding of a principle I got quite early in life kept driving me till I got to that stage. It is that same understanding I want to drive into you in this book.

I quite understand it is not everyone who will do what I do, but you can also prepare yourself and work hard. You can prepare yourself so that your net worth can increase. I worked hard so that my wife wouldn't have to work.

It's not just cooking I decided long ago that my wife wouldn't do, I also decided she would not have to work for any other man in her life. She may work if she chooses to, but she wouldn't have to work for survival. She would not have to go to work because she needs to pay 50% of the home keeping bill. She wouldn't have to work to support the family. She wouldn't have to toil for anything. That was why I worked extremely hard all my life.

Concerning cooking, I have some good friends who disagree with my point of view. Many think I prohibit my wife from cooking, my wife cooks leisurely sometimes especially when she wants to eat what our cooks cannot make. Sometimes she wants to relax by cooking, that is different.

My wife drives sometimes which I can also do. However, it is not about its prohibition. The main point of that illustration is simple; net worth.

IT'S ABOUT BUILDING AND
INCREASING NET WORTH

If you want to cook, please go ahead. Let me emphasize to you the main point one more time; Net worth. Except we understand what net worth truly means and how to create and increase net worth, it will be extremely difficult for you to agree with me on this issue. I hope over the next pages to help you see why creating net worth is of higher priority than cooking, driving or washing dishes.

You must not miss this essential point in your life. Without net worth, life would be worthless, simple and of no value.

There is a principle of life which I came to understand and of course which informed making some of this strange decisions I have discussed with you. The principle is this **"It is good to use the most part of your day where you are most effective"**. Do you get that?

Now, how does my wife not cooking and how does

my hiring drivers increase our net worth? That will take us to another very important subject matter called time.

You see everything in this life is quantified by time. Your life is quantified by time and my life is quantified by time. We all are rated and quantified by time. That is why in the business world, you have a value right now. We can measure how much you are worth in an hour. How do we do this? Because we can measure your productivity within one hour. We can measure how productive you are, you can measure what values and goods you have produced, we can quantify the services you render. We can rate you. If you want to know how much you are worth in an hour, let us look at the last one hour of your life that just passed now? How much value did you bring forth?

When I understood this principle properly, I had an idea of what one hour of my life could be worth. I began to double up my efforts on the amount of values I could birth within one hour. I knew one hour of my life was too precious to be spent driving and that of my wife too costly to be spent cooking. We could pay people whose primary calling are in those areas while we also give ourselves maximally to what we do best. We both began to harness how much value we could give birth to within an hour. The results we got was shocking, hence my passion in writing this book for you right now.

You see my friend, time is life. Time is passing away every second like water dripping away from a jug. Imagine having a jug of water with you right now on one hand and a cup on the other hand. Now picture water dripping from that jug into that cup all the while without stopping. That is how life is pouring out. That is how my life is slipping off, that is how your time and life too is slipping off. None of us can escape it.

A lot of people wander off in life without account-ability for their time or their worth, they give a portion of themselves to everything and a portion of themselves to nothing. Consequently, their lives have no conse-quence, weight or results. This is the life majority of our world live. What a pity.

3 WAYS YOU COULD SPEND YOUR LIFE

Let me mention here briefly three ways you could spend your time, consequently your life. Much details and emphasis will be laid on this discussion in a later chapter of this book. However, for a brief mention there are different things you could use life for. In fact, there are three major ways time and life could be spent. First, you could waste life like failures do. Secondly, you could spend life like a mediocre. The third and final is that you can convert your life into major solid life investments.

In my own case, I happen to think that cooking is one of the least things for my own wife. When I met my wife, what attracted her to me was not her cooking skills. In fact, I never got to eat anything she cooked until much later. When I met her, whether she could cook or not was immaterial to me. I saw splendor in my wife, I saw grace, I saw potential. Then, I took it upon myself to cultivate all of her potential into manifested wealth and self-worth. I discovered that the best place where that would be culti-vated would not be in the kitchen. I understood what an hour of being in the kitchen could do. I had the option; a good food or a purposeful wife. I chose the latter. Now, by her worth, an hour of my wife's time can successfully pay cooks for our family for an entire week.

This is what all great men know. This is the main reason people of influence do not drive their own cars or cook their own food. It is not just mere opulence or affluence. No, there is a purpose behind it. They can see the bigger picture, they see clearer. A man of worth and significance understands his worth and the advantage of increasing his net worth. He knows his worth in an hour can pay his driver or chauffeur for an entire month. That time while his chauffeur drives him from place to place, he is busy using the time to create wealth.

The poor look at the life of the rich as mere affluence or opulence. No, the rich understand strategy and the skill of constantly increasing self-worth.

For some other women, cooking is a way that could bring the best value out of them to the world. Many women have found purpose and calling in cooking and by all means must be encouraged. Some women are so gifted and purposeful with cooking, spending the rest of their lives doing it is no problem.

My wife however brings value to the world in other areas outside cooking, cooking is not her primary calling. I in same vein bring value to the world on other scales other than driving. We choose to focus and concentrate on those areas where we are strongest and best. We channel all of our energy into the direction where we can get the ultimate returns and fulfillment.

A lot of people put in all of their energy into investments that have no value. Imagine a man who wants to be a soccer star spending his entire day at the beach swimming. Though he is putting his strength, energy and focus into something good, he can as well forget about being a soccer star. That kind of investment will not bring him the best return.

YOUR TIME IS AN INVESTMENT

Your time is your most important asset and investment in life. When you put in your time into the wrong investment, there will be no results. When all of your day is spent driving when your call is not to be a driver, how can you have gains and meaningful returns? How can you be a person of worth?

Also, the rich understand that time must be gained at any cost. People of worth will spend any amount to be able to recover or buy to themselves more amount of time. The average man thinks money over gains, but the successful people think about gains over money.

What do I mean? The successful people will pay anyone any amount they need to pay them in order to buy some time for themselves. They will then use that time to create value for themselves increasing their self-worth.

The unsuccessful man however does not know this secret. His priority is money, his goal is money. He could work several hours in return for peanuts. He could spend his entire life in a month working for salary. He works with all might and no brain. What a wretched life.

In the illustration I used earlier, some women derive their ultimate fulfillment from cooking and I must emphasize that such women should be encouraged, my wife and I have lots of cooks in our house and they do their work as a calling and ministry unto people. That is what they have discovered about themselves and that is what they serve to the world.

While I do not say women should not cook, everyone makes their choice. The point remains the same, each person should and must maximize their time. You must serve yourself to the world in the areas of your greatest potential.

Another example I love to use is the time people spend in public transport. Same time is being expended by everyone within a train or subway. A person of value in a train could be reading trying to add more value to himself while another person could be writing trying to create value. However, you will discover that majority of people on that bus are just staring at nothing in particular, talking carelessly or totally lacking respect for the passing time. Do you remember our illustration of the water dripping away continuously from a jug? Such lives are like water dripping away from a jug. No value. What a waste.

What I am saying is this, that same one hour on the bus can be used to create a higher value. Let me stress the point so it cannot be missed, our net worth is determined by the value that is created within an hour of your day. That is one of the greatest truths every human being on earth should know. If you really want to be successful, then you must pay attention to that statement. In fact, this is among the biggest factors that separate all men in life, the successful from the unsuccessful. Here is the statement again, **"your net worth is determined by the value that is created within an hour of your day"**. Therefore, every hour of your day is determined by what value you create. Some people do not even pay attention to the value of one hour.

Have you heard a speaker is being paid five thousand dollars for speaking for one hour at a conference? Have you ever heard a comedian could be paid ten thousand dollars for a show? Perhaps you have hard how musicians and singers are paid several millions of dollars for few hours of performance at a concert? Do you wonder why soccer stars are not being paid same amount? Some earn ridiculous amount for playing a single match. What they are being paid for is not just their skill. Skill? Yes but much more important than that they are being paid for their value, for their value and contribution to the game. The term in the business world is called net worth. That is how the world, the entire world rates them. They are being appreciated for developing themselves, they are being thanked for their ability to bring pleasure to mankind through what they do and how they do it.

WHAT IS YOUR CURRENT NET WORTH?

I know you were probably hoping and praying that I wouldn't ask, but let me ask you right now, what is your net worth? How much are you worth? What is the value of an hour of your time? When a man has not consciously created and recreated himself, when a man has not increased his net worth and value, such a man is a waste. We all were born same, nakedly coming out of our mother's womb, but few people among us when they got to the world recreated themselves. By recreation I mean, they worked extremely hard to add value to themselves, to become a person of worth. Examples of such men include names like Richard Branson. Others you might have heard about are Aliko Dangote, Bill Gates, Warren Buffet and the list goes on and on.

I am teaching you to create the best value from your one hour. If the best value from you is to cook, then go ahead. You must cook in a way that there will be no other cook in the world who can cook like you. You must cook in a pattern that the world will give up anything to taste your dishes. You must cook with such enthusiasm and passion that generation of cooks after you will wish they met you. You must generate such value and worth that the whole world cannot deny or despise.

In my own family, I have discovered the best way to create values. The best way for my wife to create value is not to cook, but to create value in other areas. We have discovered what we do best and we expend our lives in those areas and projects. Now, my wife has added so much value in herself that today she has worldwide influence. She is being invited to speak all over the world on different subjects. She has so much value coming forth from her that people want to listen to her again and again. It did not come that easy, she labored and toiled, creating value in herself in the best area possible for her.

Another area in which she has created immense value is in adding value to our children. The time she invests in our children is of higher value, worth and significance than to invest same time in cleaning, scrubbing and washing.

WHAT ARE YOUR DAILY PRIORITIES?

The most important lesson if the focus will not be shifted is about comparative advantage. Compare what you do daily and think about your priorities. What are some of the things that if you do today will give you the biggest leverage in life? Comparative advantage states that not everything is of equal value in life.

Let me explain it to you again this way. A successful man understands comparative advantage and uses it to his gain. A successful man is never busy because he decides a few things he wants to do in a day and simply does the few that will give him the best profits and returns. A successful man could focus on just one thing or task in a day and will not back out till it is done. That is comparative advantage. We have heard stories of people who could condense all their activities into one task and will focus on just one thing for many years till they achieve it.

Poor, ignorant and unsuccessful men on the other hand are always busy. Activity does not always equate productivity. Unsuccessful people do not understand comparative advantage. They want to get so many things done. They are always moving from pillar to post, all motion no goals. Such a pattern is a waste of life, time and resources.

When you ask many men who they are and what they do, they cannot define it. They are like the ancient saying which goes thus 'jack of all trade, master of none'.

So what is comparative advantage and how does comparative advantage work? The law of Comparative advantage says that we all have same time and time can be used up for anything, however it is not everything that has equal results. Are you confused? Do not be, let me explain it to you brilliantly.

This is the point about comparative advantage. The same amount of time, same one hour or sixty minutes as you may choose to call it is given to all men. That time could be invested in the laboratory, or in the cure for cancer. It could be invested in walking in the park and merely sightseeing. Same one hour could be spent at the stadium or on the beach leisurely. Here is the kicker, the cure for cancer seems to me to give more value than just walking leisurely through a park. I hope you understand it now. What is it that you must do that will give you the best return, value and investment on your time?

As a teacher, what would you rather do that will give you fulfillment and higher return and what other activities would just be a waste of your time? As a doctor, how best can you invest your life and how best can your time be wasted? Write them down. If you practice law and stand before judges, what must you do daily? What will make you the best and give you the best yield, possibly sit in the judges' seat one day? Also, what are the things that will not add anything to you? You must note them and identify them. Same is true for all men, for all professions, for barbers as well as businessmen, for farmers and students. What will give you a comparative advantage?

HOW ARE YOU USING YOUR TIME?

While a person invests his one hour productively, another could waste his carelessly. Let us take two scientists working on a research project for example. Let us assume they have same topic and are working on same thing. One of them could spend an hour studying, researching, observing and experimenting while the other person could take same time to wash plates or to cook. Of course, cooking is not bad but if I need to choose what to use my one hour for, I will rather use my one hour to find the cure for cancer in the laboratory than to walk in the park or wash plates. A lot of things may not be bad, but they do not have same value. A lot of things you do right now are not bad, but have you thought about the value? Do they add equal value to you?

If I have a responsibility to my family and people under my influence to maximize their potential, I must open their eyes to see the best way to create their net worth. The best way is to create a net worth in their sphere of influence. The best way is to discover that which you do best and you have passion for and do it with all your strength, grace and finesse.

Now, I am sure you understand that the most important thing in life is to create maximum value. You must strive to create the maximum value in your one hour. Since you understand now that your net worth is determined by how much value you can create within your one hour, what will you begin to do differently?

Another question for you is this, how can you create the maximum value for yourself in one hour? How do you increase your net worth? I will bring you so much light and illumination in this regard soon.

This is the idea, the difference between people and their net worth is in the value that they create. I'm not talking about your network. So much is being said today about network, many of which are undisputedly true.

Network refers to who you know and who recommends you. But, a solid way to beat network all the time is through your net worth. In other words, a man with a strong net worth will always win over a man with a strong network.

An example is this, a man with a strong network will get a good job, that's no doubt. But he will only get the job because a man with a strong net worth created the company. A man with a strong net worth does not need to look for recommendations or who will favor him, he converts his net worth into whatever he needs per time.

Your net worth and value and respect and honor is in what you are able to produce in an hour of your time. How much value are you able to create within an hour of your time. How much value are you able to create in an hour of your day? The only thing many people achieve within an hour of their day is that they visited the toilet. When all a man achieved in an hour was that he passed feces, what will you describe his worth as? Your guess is as good as mine.

YOUR NET WORTH IS DECIDED BY WHAT YOU DO IN AN HOUR

Let us imagine this for a moment. Let us take eight hours as the standard working hour of a day. The average working time around the world in a day is eight hour. What is your net worth in an hour?

Again, your net worth is decided by what you do in an hour of your life, I mean each hour of your life. Each hour is deciding your net worth, your value. Each hour is deciding your future. In fact each hour is actually painting the picture of your whole life. What will you do with your passing time? What will you do with your passing hour?

Like I wrote earlier, one hour of your life and how you spend one day of your life is the picture of your life. If you can afford to waste one hour, you can waste the whole day. If you can waste hours, you can waste a day without noticing it or feeling anything amiss. The way you spend one day is a picture of your whole life.

Therefore, if you are prone to wasting time. If you are prone to watching your life drip away like water from a jug, if you are prone to not creating value within an hour of your day, it means your whole life will not be of value. You will be shocked to suddenly wake up one day and it's your sixtieth birthday. Hurray, the only thing you would have achieved is that your life has now been placed on pension.

The only thing people on pension have done with their life is that they gave their time and youth to somebody else, to the government. If you live your life like that, the only thing you will do with your life is that you had a job and you lived on salary. Salary is the monetary compensation for your life and time you willingly gave away. Like the water in the jug in our illustration, many people on salary are merely being poured out, they are simply wasting away.

Why? It is definitely not because God does not love you. It is also not that God hates you or that life is not fair, it is because you lived a lifestyle that is not used to creating value in an hour. Anyone that is not used to creating value within an hour of his day will be shocked at the end of his life. There will be nothing to show for it. And the reason is not because Satan is bad or that God is not blessing him, it is just because they have not mastered the wealth of time. They have not planned to master life and they have not mastered the secret of conversion. Such people have not learnt conversion and they have not learned the secret of maximizing their life or how to form their net worth. They have not learnt how to use their life to create a system of value chain. We will look critically on the subject of creating value chains in the next chapters.

When a man has not learnt the principle of creating value for every hour, his life has not become valuable nor can it exist in a value chain. Due to this reason, such a man merely thinks the most important thing in his life is getting a good job. Getting a good job is mortgaging your life. The greatest thing about your life is not your job, it is your assignment, work, calling and purpose on the earth. It is for what reason you have been configured and the problem you were sent to the earth to solve. A lot of people in life give this up in exchange for survival and peanuts they are given at the end of every month. At the end they give you pension, which is basically saying to you **'Go and die'**

Pension is saying 'Thanks, we got your best years from you, now retire and let your children do same for us. The slavery where you have served and the bondage you have served is also reserved, it is still here waiting for your children. Give your children too an opportunity to enroll'.

Then your children, when they have not been trained differently will also work for salary, your children's-children also. This is a tragedy. It beats my mind that this is the way many people live their lives today. In fact, it is not just the way many people live their life, but that is also the way several generations before them lived. Except such people are delivered by such a book and material as this, several generations after them stand at risk also.

DON'T LIVE YOUR BEST YEARS
IN SERVITUDE

I once met a man working on a government job who was so proud to tell me that his forefathers served on same job and same office. I wish he understood what he was saying but he did not. This man was simply saying his forefathers and himself have perfected the art of servitude. They have been enrolled into a life of trans-generational slavery. Except he has a mental shift and a change of perspective, the fate of his children unborn could have been determined already.

Do I have anything against working on government jobs and private companies, collecting salaries? Not necessarily so. But I am totally against working on a job that does not allow you create value. I am against you spending eight hours every day in places where your productivity is undermined and undervalued. I am against you living like ants, from hands to mouth. I am against you working when the sole reason you are on the job is for survival. I am against anything that does not bring out the best in you or maximize your potential.

When you put all of this together, you will discover that there is probably no work anyone can create for you that can truly maximize your potential except the one you create for yourself. What do you think? I will be surprised if you agree otherwise.

A life based on a job and salary is not a good life and it is not the best life. I am trying to get your mind to wrap around what the best life is for you. I am talking about a full life and being in charge of your life.

For you to be in charge of your life, then you must be in charge of your seconds, minutes and hours. Let me put it another way, for you to truly be in charge of your life, then you must be able to determine the outcome of every single moment of your life. You must be accountable for every single second and moment of your day. You must be able to account for every hour of your life. Every hour of your day must be creating a definite value, every hour of your day must give the world a tangible value and worth. You must strive within every hour to either add value to yourself, add value to others or create a product of value.

So dear friend, having known this that you just read, what are you going to do about it? How are you going to begin to create your net worth? How will you begin to derive value for each hour of your life? How can you optimize your life span and existence on the earth?

I have a passion, and that is not to see a single second of my life wasted. Yes, I mean not a single second. I understand that every time I have on the earth is an investment and what I do with it is my responsibility. What you do with your own time too is your responsibility.

Wake up, don't waste away, do not drip away, like the water in the jug continuously dripping off into oblivion.

HIGHLIGHTS
FROM CHAPTER TREE

1. Without net worth, life would be worthless, simple and of no value.

2. It is good to use the most part of your day where you are most effective

3. Everything in this life is quantified by time. Your life is quantified by time and my life is quantified by time.

4. A lot of people wander off in life without accountability for their time or their worth, they give a portion of themselves to everything and a portion of themselves to nothing.

5. There are three major ways time and life could be spent. First, you could waste life like failures do. Secondly, you could spend life like a mediocre. The third and final is that you can convert your life into major solid life investments.

6. A lot of people put in all of their energy into investments that have no value.

7. The rich understand that time must be gained at any cost. People of worth will spend any amount to be able to recover or buy to themselves more amount of time.

8. The average man thinks money over gains, but the successful people think about gains over money.

CHAPTER 4

··

CREATING AND BUILDING YOUR NET WORTH

In the last chapter, we discussed extensively on what it means to have a net worth. We were also able to critically consider time as the basic element of building your net worth.

Having understood that, I am going to discuss with you in this new chapter how to create and build your net worth. I am going to begin to share with you basic tools and principles for conversion of your time into net worth.

Already, you understand the value of time to building your net worth. I am sure you clearly remember that without value for time, there will be no value for life or existence.

Do you still remember our example of the jug full of water continuously dripping away into a cup or bowl? Yes, I am sure you remember. That is how everyone's life is continuously dripping away. You cannot stop it, it's how life runs. It is how life is built to run.

As you are reading this book now, time is passing away. Time was passing away when you were sleeping, time was dripping off while you were driving and cooking, time was dripping away when you were watching television.

I know you have often wished to stop the clock so that it would not run and you would have enough time to do what you wanted to do. You are not alone, I have severally wished so too, same with every man who has lived on the earth. However, stopping time is what no man, no scientist, magician or miracle worker has ever succeeded to do in the world. Time is running and it is running very fast.

So how can you maximize time? What can you do to get the best out of your passing time?

HOW TO USE YOUR TIME EFFECTIVELY

There are 3 major ways by which time can be used effectively.

1. Invest time in yourself:

Only few people invest quality time in themselves yet it remains one of the best uses of time. Time invested in yourself can be converted to becoming anything. When time is put into yourself for constructive purposes, only then can you become a person of worth and value.

A lot of people in the world today spend time while many more waste their time. A person of worth however creates a good time for self-development. When I came to understand this truth, I made solid and concrete decisions about my life. When I clearly understood that it is the worth that you put within yourself that can only come out of you, my life changed drastically.

I converted this time of self-investment into moments of solitude and my moments of solitude into moments of value. I decided to create a week of solitude for myself every month, and I have done this consistently for the last twenty years.

If you want to know the secret of Pastor Sunday, that is one right there. My week of solitude is a week I do not come in contact with anyone but just being away, learning, studying and meditating.

You see it is impossible to become anything tangible in life in the midst of the ever busy and buzzing moments of life without taking time away for solitude. Apart from taking a week off to be in solitude every month, I have consistently practiced the art of self-study for a period of three to six hours every day since I was in the University. People of worth are people who study, people of value are people who create the time to be alone in self-meditation, self-study and solitude.

A computer programming language says garbage in, garbage out. It is whatever you put within yourself that can only come out of you when you are under pressure.

2. Invest time in others.

People of worth and value add value to others. Adding value to other people and to your world is the great use of life. When you are not adding value to others, you are merely living for yourself and to only live for oneself is death.

If there are men whose names ring for their impact and contribution in their generation, it is because such men created the time to add value in other people.

As a leader, if you will not be forgotten the same moment you are dead, you must consciously begin to add value to other people today. You must start nurturing young people and pouring yourself into them.

As a parent, if you want your future to be secured and the generations after you secured, you must begin to create time and value in your children.

It is so sad today that a lot of parents have no time for their children. A lot of children see less of their own parents, while clients and customers see more of such parents in their offices and places of work. What a misplacement of priority. I once read the sad story of a young boy who offered to pay for an hour of his dad's time.

The story line is about a man who always comes home from work late, tired and irritated. The night the event I am about to describe happened was not the first time he was coming back late, he came home late every day. However, this particular night he found his 5 year old son waiting for him at the door.

"Daddy, may I ask you a question?"

"Yeah, sure, what is it?" replied the man.

"Daddy, how much money do you make an hour?"

"That's none of your business! What makes you ask such a thing?" the man said angrily.

"I just want to know. Please tell me, how much do you make an hour?" pleaded the little boy.

"If you must know, I make $20.00 an hour."

"Oh," the little boy replied, head bowed.

Looking up, he said, "Daddy, may I borrow $20.00 please?"

"Why do you want the money and what will you use the money for?" the father grumbled.

"Because I want to buy an hour of your day tomorrow," the little boy replied.

"Daddy, can I have $20.00 now. Can I buy an hour of your time tomorrow?"

If you had to choose, would you rather choose to have

more money or a great future for your children? Think about it.

Statistics says almost 72% of African-American children are growing up without the presence of a father. These set of children have been described as a high risk group for Prostitution, Thuggery and armed robbery including many other vices.

A staggering 85% of young men in prisons are said to have grown up in homes without the presence of a father and almost all of the prisoners in prisons lacked proper parental care growing up.

Please think about this again.

Again, when we live for ourselves, we die. But a life that is well invested in other people is a great life. My life has been that of constantly pouring out of myself into other people. I have come to understand the value that people hold and there is no way I can treat anyone lesser than they deserve.

I have seen people move from the sidewalks of life into the main spot. I have picked people off the streets, alcoholics and drunkards, men that the whole world had completely given up on. I have spent a great deal of my life cleaning such men and cultivating their potential. Today, many of these people are successful business men, top parliamentarians, politicians and diplomats. I have seen the incredible things that can happen when we add value to people. There is no purer joy, no better way to expend life.

3. Create a product:

While it is really excellent to add value to yourself and add value to other people, the third and very important way to use your time is to create products of value.

Every product that we make use of today was produced by somebody. In other words, someone spent an incredible moment of their lives to produce what is today called the computer, the telephone, the IPad, wrist-watches etc. In fact, this book you are holding right now is a product of time and time well invested. The products you generate show what your true value is. A man who has no product has no value.

When you have products of value, you can solve problems in different parts of the world simultaneously. Your presence can be felt at same time in different regions and continents of the world at the same time. You can be in the United States helping people to get through life and at the same time be in Nigeria influencing people. Your products can duplicate you.

Steve Jobs gave the world the IPad. His IPad is today in millions of homes solving many problems. Everywhere you see an IPad, you have seen a Steve Jobs. That is what your product can do for you. Do not die barren. Do not die fruitless. Do not die without using your time to birth something that the world can remember you for.

THE PRODUCTS YOU MAKE BUILD YOU A NET WORTH

Long after you are gone from the surface of the earth, your product will still continue to live on the earth. Hence the only way to keep living after death, the only way to keep speaking after death and the only way to keep influencing people after your death is through your product. I have written entire books on this subject of conversion and how you build products that will outlive you for thousands of years.

If you must increase your net worth, you must seek to convert your time into products.

The Net worth of Bill Gates today is said to be 76 billion dollars. What they are really saying is that his product, his company, Microsoft is valued at around same amount. When successful men would increase their net worth, they create new products, they build new companies. It is only unsuccessful people and people with poverty mind-set who think they can increase their net worth by getting better paying jobs or seeking new salaries.

Seek to build your net worth by building products. Seek to increase your net worth by converting your time into products of value. What goods and services can you render? What value can you give? What creativity can you bring to a value that is being given already? How can you do old things in a new way? These are questions you must always ask yourself if you must come up with new products.

Additionally, if you must constantly come up with new products, you must understand systems. Many people marvel when I tell them I write at least one book per week. They simply cannot fathom it. But the secret is in systems. With systems you can rain down products on the earth until the entire earth is soaked with your ideas. You can let the world get soaked with what you offer that they find you in every street corner or in every home in the world. The power of systems makes you do that.

An example is the McDonalds food chain. McDonalds began as an idea of two brothers which they started at the back of the house. Today, McDonalds is found in most major cities around the world. What took an idea from the backyard into international recognition? The taste of burgers? Not necessarily that, it is the power of a good system. The McDonald system has successfully launched and turned the McDonald brothers' ideas into a global and world-wide vision.

Finally, it is either you are adding value to yourself or you are adding value to others or you are creating value into some goods or services. If you are not monitoring every hour of your day, if you cannot account for everything that you do for every hour of your day, then your net worth will be empty. If you cannot account for what value you create every hour, then your value will be zero upon the earth, your net worth will be absolutely nothing, you will become bankrupt.

A man who has no value for time will be a worker for the rest of his life, he will just be on salary for the rest of his period on the surface of the earth living from hands to mouth.

Such a man will be a pathetic sight at the end of his life because he is not converting his life into worth and net worth. Such a man is not converting his life into value.

When you live your life purposelessly without judicious use of each hour, then you are not creating a value chain for yourself, you have become a victim of life.

THE GREATEST WEALTH IN LIFE IS TIME

The greatest wealth in life is not salary or job or money, the greatest wealth in life and the greatest resource in life is time. Let me help you understand those words very clearly. You see, my dear friend, the man who has just money is not really wealthy. Money is just a material, an expression of wealth. But the man who has time has wealth because time is wealth. This is why every day, every man is equally wealthy. God made it that way in order to be a just God.

Let me use this illustration to help you understand it better. Let us assume we both are given two small tins of maize seeds to do anything we desire with. Let us assume none of us is instructed on what to do with the seeds we are given. You may decide to cook yours and eat. When you have the maize seeds prepared as food, even though you have the physical food, you are still poor. You are still poor because though the maize seeds could become food, it is not the best use at that particular time.

Now Imagine that I immediately seek out the best soil for my own seeds and I immediately begin putting the seeds into the ground, though at that point in time, I may appear poor and hungry, but I am truly wealthy.

Same is with money and wealth. Money is a form of wealth but is not the strongest form of wealth. Time is the strongest form of wealth. Time is the strongest form of wealth because your time can be converted into whatever you want it to be converted into. Time can be converted into money, time can be converted into building, time can be converted into goods and services, time can be converted into influence, time can be converted into cars, houses, lands etc. Time can be converted into whatever you desire for it to become. Here comes one of the greatest words again to learn in life; the word conversion.

The greatest thing you could discover in life is conversion, the greatest word to learn in life is the word conversion. You must know and learn the secret of conversion.

Conversion is bringing every minute, second, hour

and day into account and value. It is optimizing your day. It is the ability to look at the moment that just went by and show to us what you made from that moment, what did you achieve? What did you produce?

If you can become a master in converting your time into value, you can become anything that you want to become. Anyone can become anything they want to become if they can discover the value of time. Time is wealth, time is resource, time is more than money, time is life. If you learn to convert time into anything you want to convert it into, you can become whatever it is that you want to become.

EVERYTHING IS A PRODUCT OF TIME

Everything that we see today is a product of time, everything is made from a certain use of time. Time creates everything. Everything you see now is a product of time. Every child is a product of time, every adult is a product of time, even you are a product of time.

If you didn't stay in the womb of your mother for 9 months, you would not have been alive today. In spite of how your parents or family try, if you won't be in the womb for 9 months, you would not have been seen on the earth today. It is that time of incubation that created you. You are a product of time. You are a creation of time. You will not be working or talking today if not for the value of time.

Everything on earth today is put under the value of time.

When you give birth to a child, within 3 months, the child is already making attempts to sit down. This is not just happening because you are in Europe or Africa, it is happening same way everywhere including America, Asia and Australia. It does not matter the color of skin or the part of the world, something happens to the child in 3 months. 3 months creates value in a child that the whole world can see and appreciate. In 3 months the value of sitting is created in the child.

After a period of about 6 months, this child begins to crawl. Where did that ability come from? Still time. It is the time that has created that value and ability. The period of 6 months has provided within the child certain grace and that grace and ability makes the child begin to crawl after the defined time.

Everything is created from time. That is a Universal principle. Everything that got created got created because of time. In fact, time creates everything. Still talking about the child in our earlier example, when it is about one year, the child begins to walk. Do you see that?

Everything is made out of time. My IPad is a product of time. It is a product of time invested in creating it. When you buy anything in the store, you are not paying for the thing specifically, you are paying for the time in producing that thing. The price tag is not just about the raw material that was used in producing it, you are paying for the time that the manufacturer used in producing that product and of course the time it took him to acquire the needed skill to make such a product.

You are paying for the time of the people who worked to produce it. You are paying for the time of the people who came up with the idea. You are paying for the time the manufacturers spent in doing research and in adding value to themselves. This is why you are paid a salary for a time. Usually salary is paid within a month.

When you are paid a salary, it means you gave a month of your life for the exchange of the money you are paid. It is an exchange. For example, if you are paid three hundred dollars at the end of the month as salary, you are only being given that amount for a month-worth of your life.

Again, everything is a product of time. My house was built in 9 months, it could not have been built in 2 days. Everything is time. Time is the raw material from which everything is created. Time is the source from which everything is created. Therefore, if time is so important, it means you can take a hold of time and decide to become anything you want to become.

I once spoke to people about knowing a group of friends in my childhood. They were a group of seven friends who were always together and who did everything together. They decided to make something tangible out of themselves within a period of 6 years.

Six years later, 5 of them decided to convert that period of time into products and values. They had an engineer and a doctor among them. They took hold of the time they had and through labor and through hard work converted the time into whoever they wanted to become. One of them who wanted to become an engineer converted the time in the school of engineering and became an engineer. The one who wanted to become a medical doctor spent same amount of time in the medical school, converted the knowledge in the time through work and through studying into achieving his dream. They became lawyers, doctors, engineers etc. Could they have swapped professions? Yes, they could have swapped. All that was needed also was a change in the conversion process. They applied time into a conversion process and became who they sought out to become.

WITH TIME, YOU CAN BUILD, ACHIEVE OR BECOME ANYTHING

All that is needed is taking the time that is available and converting your time into an added value. You decide what value you want to add to yourself.

I once shared that those childhood friends could have become anything that they wanted. It is easier and more pleasurable, satisfying and fulfilling if you first of all find out what your calling is. If you are called to be an engineer, you must be careful not to convert your time to becoming a medical doctor. You will not be as satisfied, as fulfilled if you are converting yourself into someone or something else. If you are called to be an engineer and you got to convert your time into your area of calling, then it gives you more fulfillment and more joy.

You are exactly like a fish in the river. You run and accomplish easily within your natural sphere. You do everything with grace and ease.

If you are called to be an engineer for example but you are forcing your way in conversion through medicine, then you are swimming against the tide. You are like a drowning lion. A lion is struggling for survival within the water, not because its gene or its strength has waned. A lion's biggest struggle in water is because it is out of its strength zone. Many people are out of their strength zone in life. They live each day out of their strength zone, they operate everyday with depleted energy. They totally lack focus. There is no way such a life can be productive.

Here is the beautiful thing. You can convert time

to become anything. If you can master time and every moment of your day, then you can decide whatever it is that you want to become. There will be no stopping you. You can become anything.

HOW DO YOU BUILD YOUR NET WORTH?

Let me give you some concrete points and give you more concrete facts. What I am about to tell you will elevate you and cause your net worth to increase. When you pay attention to this that I raise, there is no doubt that you will be on your way to the top.

Again, here is the question, in a day, in an hour how do you increase your net worth? Let me begin by telling you the most important thing in this your new found journey; discover your calling.

Yes, find out what your calling is: The first thing to do in order to increase your net worth is to discover your calling on the earth. While entire books have been dedicated to this subject and I have many books on this topic myself, I want to help you discover your calling in this book in simple terms. I want to help you discover that which your purpose is without much hassle. I want to help you locate what you were born to do.

In order to discover your calling, you must learn to pay a great deal of attention to yourself. You must learn to listen to the whispers of your own heart. You must learn to be real and passionate to live out your own life on the earth and not somebody else's life. It is so sad today that a greater majority of our world today are caught up in somebody else's life and somebody else's business. Such people went to school for the reason that someone suggested it to them, studied a particular program in the university because it was somebody else's desire for them. Eventually when many people graduate from college, they take up jobs which are so far away from their own desire.

An average human being spends more than two-thirds of his entire life trying to please people or somebody else. Many people do not really get to live, they only exist, they only survive.

A man who will increase his net worth however must be very restless until he has discovered his calling and has found himself right in the middle of it.

So how do you discover your calling and how do you start living within your calling? If you must discover your calling, then endeavor to note and identify now: what are your passions, what do you have the strong affinity for? What makes you concerned all day and embitters your heart? What gives you joy and gladdens your heart? What do you want to see happen for people? What are some of those things that you can do all day? Have you discovered what your talents are? What gives you boundless energy and you can continue to do without being paid? When you are able to answer some or all of these questions, there is no doubt that you would have identified, discovered and can effectively live out your calling.

Calling is generic and it is specific. It is generic because everyone has a call. It is specific because no one has same call as you do. Hence, no one can effectively tell you all that you are designed for, it is what you will have to discover for yourself.

SELF-DISCOVERY MAKES YOU RELEVANT TO THE WORLD

You have to discover yourself and your calling. Self-discovery is what makes you relevant to your world. It is the expression of your purpose and calling on earth that gives you a name on the earth.

I don't know what names you think you bear. The only names most people carry around are the names given by their parents. But your real name on the earth is by the assignment and the purpose you fulfill.

For example, I might not mention the anti-apartheid struggle, but simply mentioning Nelson Mandela defines it. Everyone knows what I'm talking about. That was the name that Mandela bore. He was not just carrying Nelson around and we begin to wonder which of the Nelsons he is. Same way, when I mention about human right activism in America and the liberation of the blacks, you would almost immediately talk to me about Martin Luther King. King had a name because he fulfilled a purpose and an assignment.

Your calling and assignment will give you a name on the earth. What are your natural talents? What are your natural abilities? What are some of those things you can do without being taught? Answers to all of these will show you the weapons you have in your arsenal with which you can conquer in your lifetime.

When you have discovered what your calling is, then you have to make sure you are converting every minute and every hour of your day into adding value in your area of calling. In one hour, you must ask yourself this question, what am I doing right now that is adding value to me in regards to my calling? What am I doing that is making me better? This information that I'm going to acquire, this meeting I'm going to? How is this thing that am exposed to going to help me to fulfill my calling? How can I use it and convert this information into making me become whom I'm supposed to become? How can this thing be used?

Imagine having me in a room where there is a lot of light, now imagine also that the light is not hot neither can it cut through glass. If you take that same light and use laser and the power of a laser to bring it into a focus, if you turn same amount of energy of laser to convert it into a single focus, imagine the power that light will have.

If you focus the energy that is just giving light, the energy that is otherwise powerless and ineffective, if you turn that same amount of energy through a laser, it becomes extra-ordinary. When that energy is applied and brought into focus through the power of a laser, it could become like hot fire. It will cut through anything. It will become an energy like the light the welders and iron cutters use. It could break through any iron, because it is focused.

Same thing happens when you convert your energy and time into a concrete specific area of calling. When you know your area of calling, then you are laser effective. When you begin to ask the right questions? When you ask questions that will bring you lot of benefit, questions such as *'this information that I am reading now, how can I use it to advance myself in my area of calling? How can I use it to advance and further myself within the area of my calling? How can it help me to become better? How can I be more valuable in everything that I do?'*

When you ask questions like this, you begin to avoid distractions as much as possible. You will not be a party of endless, unproductive meetings. Every single hour of your day will have meaning to you and you will convert it to add lot of value to yourself. You become a conscious person who pays attention to every single minute that is in your day.

That means you are concentrating all the energy into laser focus. The result is not just going to be some lazy results, rather your effectiveness will soar and become higher. When you are working and you are converting every minute into benefits. When you are actively developing within your calling, when every activity is targeted towards improving yourself, then you are already increasing your net worth in that one hour.

The difference between people is in what they do in an hour

Let me remind you that difference between people is not in race, color, country or economy, height or size. The major difference between people is in what they do in an hour. What amount of value they are able to produce within an hour of their day. The difference between people and their net worth is in what they are able to produce in an hour of their day.

If we are to estimate right now, what value did you produce in the last one hour? Did you succeed in producing or in making any products? What value was added to you? Were you able to add value to anyone else? The answers you give to these questions are what determine whether you have any values or not.

If you have not been productive, what are you going

to do about it? How are you going to become more productive? Or are you just going to be like the water in the jug, just dripping away without any benefits? You can convert your time into benefits for yourself, you can convert your time into added value for others, you can also use your time to make products. You do not have to waste your life.

HIGHLIGHTS
FROM CHAPTER FOUR

1. There are 3 major ways by which time can be used effectively; Invest time in yourself, add value to others, build a product

2. When time is put into yourself for constructive purposes, only then can you become a person of worth and value.

3. As a leader, if you will not be forgotten the same moment you are dead, you must consciously begin to add value to other people today.

4. A man who has no product has no value.

5. When you have products of value, you can solve problems in different parts of the world simultaneously.

6. Do not die without using your time to birth something that the world can remember you for.

7. A man who will increase his net worth must be very restless until he has discovered his calling and has found himself right in the middle of it.

CHAPTER 5
····················

HOW TO INCREASE YOUR NET WORTH

Having learnt the principle of creating and building your net worth, let us now consider what it will take you to increase your net worth. In this chapter, I will not only share principles of increasing your net worth, but I will also share ways by which your net worth can increase continually.

You see, dear friend, it is not enough for you to create a net worth, you must find ways by which your net worth can continuously increase. You must seek strategies and ideas that can make your net worth accumulative. Did I say you must seek? Well, those strategies and ideas are within this chapter and I hope that you pay attention to every point that I have highlighted.

You cannot afford to be average, you cannot afford to be a mediocre, you cannot afford to be lesser than anything that God has made you, hence you must seek to always increase your net worth on the earth.

INCREASING YOUR NET WORTH
IS EASY, THIS IS HOW

Let us now proceed to discuss the strategy for improving your net worth. Increasing your net worth is quite easy, it begins with you discovering what your calling is as I discussed with you in the previous chapter.

After you have discovered your calling and you are growing within your calling, what comes next?

The secret to increasing your net worth is this; your net worth and the value you produce in an hour directly depends on how much value you have earlier added to yourself. How much of self-education you have acquired and how much of personal development you have done on yourself. This is why personally I do self-education a minimum of three hours every day. Many times I am in solitude everyday studying for upwards of six hours. Why am I doing this? Why am I so committed to personal development that way? It is because of a secret that I have learnt.

I have learnt that it is the amount of value you have created within yourself that will determine the amount of value you can create outside of yourself. The amount of value you have added to your mind is what determines what comes out of you.

This also determines the amount of value you can create as a concrete product. This is why it is almost impossible to see any truly successful person who is not a reader. You cannot see anyone who truly made it to the top who is not addicted to books or to reading. This is a major secret of life. I once read the story of Bill Gates, the richest man in the world where he stated he had read at least a book per week since his childhood. It is unlikely you will find a man with such a lifestyle who would not do extremely well.

Great minds are great readers and people of worth are people who are constantly adding value to themselves. You might be surprised that only a very few people in life know this. Of the very few people who know this, only a fewer percentage of people adhere to this rule and principle.

You would have raised yourself so high in the ladder of life if only you will be intentional about your self-education and self-development. You will be among the people with a very high net worth and your net worth will increase exponentially.

If you have done a lot of self-education and added value to yourself, your net worth will always grow. If you stop adding value to yourself, your net worth will also stop.

How do you add value to yourself?

So how do you add value to yourself? You add value to yourself by constantly educating yourself and looking for new opportunities that will always add to you. You add value to yourself when you choose to gather resources and materials that will increase how well you function. You add value to yourself when you choose educational programs that will help you meet the right people. You will add value to yourself when you constantly ask people around you the right questions.

Many ears ago, I decided to always intentionally ask the right questions from everyone I meet in a bid to learn something from everybody. Needless to say, that journey has been incredible for me. It has added immense value to me. I discovered that I could learn something from everybody. A lot of people talk just to communicate and pass information. Only very few people talk in order to learn and to increase their own value. The way to do that is to ensure you ask questions when you talk.

When you are constantly asking questions you will

know more. Ask people who are doing better than you good questions. Ask questions from your mentors. Everyone around me knows that they must always ask me questions, otherwise I feel there is no use being around me. Asking the right questions help you get the right answers, application of the right answers that you got will help to increase your worth and value.

In the quintessential story of Chris Garner, one of America's multi-billionaires, a single question catapulted him from life on the street to a life of influence and affluence. According to him, one day while on the street as a broke person, he happened to stumble upon a stockbroker who apparently had the kind of life he desired. He immediately proceeded to ask the man perhaps the most important question of his life up till that time, 'What is it that you do and how do you do it?'

That question made him secure an appointment with the stock broker who later brought him into the business of the stock market. The rest like they say is history. So one question for you right now, what question do you need to ask someone and when are you going to ask that question?

INCREASE YOUR NET WORTH
THROUGH DILIGENT LABOR

The next thing to do after you have discovered your calling and you have added worth to yourself through self-education is to increase your net worth through the quality of your labor. In fact, let me put it to you more accurately, one of the most important things you can do to increase your net worth is the quality of your labor.

We live today in a shallow world where a lot of people

prefer to do shoddy and shabby jobs. People who will increase their net worth however, must be people who must be ready to do their work qualitatively.

Let me remind you of this all important quote by Ralph Waldo Emerson in which he said that "If a man can write a better book, preach a better sermon, or make a better mousetrap than his neighbor, though he build his house in the woods, the world will make a beaten path to his door."

This is one quote you must strive never to forget in life if you must be a person of value. If you will ever be a person that will affect and impact the world, you must have the ideology behind that quote engraved upon your heart. Because it is very important for you to remember this point to remember, let me repeat the quote again for you in bold letters, **"If a man can write a better book, preach a better sermon, or make a better mousetrap than his neighbor, though he build his house in the woods, the world will make a beaten path to his door."**

The quality of your labor decides your net worth. The world will pay anything and any amount to a man who can not only do his job well, but who can do his job excellently well. There are doctors and there are excellent doctors, there are teachers and there are excellent teachers, there are those who call themselves engineers and there are excellent engineers, there are musicians and there are those who make the world stand still just to listen to them. What makes all the difference between these categories of people is in the quality of their work.

Talking about the quality of work, this that I am discussing with you right now is what has always amused me about many Africans. A lot of time that I have given assignments to Africans and their European counterparts, you will be shocked when you compare the results they bring to you.

I have a lot of Africans and Europeans who work with me and I discover how I have to constantly monitor and check on the work that these Africans are doing. It seems that these fellows are not able to do any quality job without being monitored and supervised. The difference is in the value system that has been set up by these individuals and societies.

I dare say that this is one of the strongest reasons Africa is the way it is today and seem to be many light years behind Europe. How do you do your job as a civil servant? What quality of work do you produce as a police man or law enforcement agent? How do you do your work as a cleaner or barber? What ratings do you have as a politician? Can we ask you to stand on same platform that we will place your counterparts from the rest of the world? Can you compete effectively with other professionals from any part of the world in what you do? What if your work were to be placed side by side and in comparison to what other people do, wouldn't you have to bury your head in shame?

(Your mantra: nobody does better than me)

As a person who will increase his net worth and value, what do you do when you know you have one hour. While a person may use an entire hour on social network, another person is working hard in a concentrated manner. At the end of the way, the two of them cannot have same net worth. It is impossible.

Quality of work increases your net worth. Like typing, someone may type 1000 words an hour while someone else may type 10, 000 words in an hour. We must pay attention to quality of work in everything we do.

How do you improve the quality of what you do? How do you become a person of quality? How do you increase your net worth through the quality of what you do? The secret lies in what I am about to tell you right now. I dare say again that applying this one thing alone is enough to separate you from the pack, this secret is big and solid enough to distinguish you from the crowd. So what is the secret of improving the quality of what you do?

PAY ATTENTION TO DETAILS

I always teach my disciples that everything depends on how you relate to small things. If there are no small things as it pertains to you, if you relate with everything diligently including the smallest of things, you will be a person of quality.

To a person of quality, there is really no small thing. There is absolutely nothing small. Excellence is in the details, in the minutest of things. Excellence is paying attention to details and paying the maximum attention to the smallest of things. That is how to improve your net worth through the quality of what you do.

Many years ago during a period of my solitude, I could audibly hear a voice in a very clear manner as if I was in a trance. The voice communicated to me 'Pay attention to details and excellence will not be an issue'.

Since then, my passion and drive is to always be the best at what I do. In fact I made a resolve, that there will be nothing I do while I am on this earth that will not be the best. There is nothing I do that will not be able to compete meaningfully with what anyone is doing at least two hundred years after I am gone.

That is, the books I write and the sermons I preach, every product I release will still be among the best decades and several years when I am no longer physically present. Nobody will out-prepare me, out-do me or out-class me. It is a resolve of excellence. That is how to improve your net worth.

There are a few names today that are known and identified with excellence, one of such names is Donald Trump, the 45th President of America. He did not just become a person of extreme worth and class in the real estate world before joining politics, he labored for it. He was a man who paid extreme attention to details. I once read one of his books where he said he personally inspects every material that will be used for any of his construction works by himself. He does this to ensure that only the very best is being used. According to him, he knows every tree that are on all of his golf courses by name, the year they were planted and what country they were brought from. You cannot have a man pay such level of attention to details and he will not be successful.

I have met a lot of people who cannot even remember what they had for lunch talk less of knowing what they did or achieved with their last paycheck.

PAY ATTENTION TO
DETAILS IN YOUR FINANCES

When it comes to paying attention to details, one major area of relevance is in your finances.

I can categorically tell you that I know what I do with my every dime. That is why I do not carry money around because each and every of my money has already gone to work for me, and I can tell you what work they are doing.

If you will not become impoverished in life, barely making it by each day, if you will not become a burden to the society and a liability to neighbors, then you must pay attention to details in your finances.

When raising people in my master classes on money, helping them to become millionaires, I task them to begin to record every money that comes into their pocket and every money that leaves their pocket and where it went. A lot of these people do not find it convenient initially, but like I always tell them, there is no other alternative to becoming a millionaire.

Many of these people became millionaires within a year of practicing this discipline. What am I saying? Only people of value practice the discipline of details.

In your marriage, are you paying attention to details? In living with your spouse and children, how attentive are you to details? Do you know what is going on in your own home?

I am amazed at men whose wives will take a full day to look good at the salon and when such wives come home, they get no appreciation or commendation from non-observing husbands. There is no way such a wife will be happy. However, when attention to details is being paid, when you notice her new dress and shoes, the make-up, the new hand bag etc, you will help her understand she is valuable to you. By so doing, you are adding a great deal of worth and value to your marriage. If you want your marriage to work, then pay attention to details. If you want to increase your net worth in the family, pay attention to details.

So, from the above paragraphs, we have carefully established that to men of worth, details and quality of work is everything. As far as such men are concerned, there are no little things, there are no unimportant things. Everything is important to them. If you do your work with the attitude of doing quality and the best things, then you are a person of worth and of value. Whatever your hands find to do, you have to do it with all your heart.

If you could do quality work or labor, then it will improve your net worth. The quality of labor you perform with your attitude to little things, will determine the heights you will attain in life. When I see anyone who can do a job excellently with great attention to details, then I can pay such a man anything for the job. When I see people who do things qualitatively, I want such people to be around me and to work with me. Unfortunately, we have only few of such people.

Many people are only waiting for the important things to come first before they give in their best and all their heart, but if you only wait for the important things to come before you work excellently, then it will never come.

So if you are not responsible and you do not do quality work in small things, you will never be able to do quality things in bigger things as well.

Conclusively, read this famous words by Martin Luther King Junior, he said *"If I cannot do great things, I can do small things in a great way"*.

INCREASE YOUR NET WORTH BY CREATING A DEMAND FOR YOURSELF

How else do you increase your net worth? When you have discovered your calling and are walking in it. When you have worked so hard on adding value to yourself. When you have become a person of skill and you are now doing very quality job. What again do you do to increase your net worth? The next most significant way to increase your net worth is by creating demand for yourself and what you do.

When you do, you increase your net worth and become a person that is highly sought after. As a speaker or author, as a writer or blogger, as a business man or professor, even as a clergy, a major way your value and net worth is estimated is by the demand for you and your product and services.

I want to teach you right now how you can increase your demand and raise how much you become sought after. I want to teach you how like they say in the business world to **"draw customers to yourself and monopolize the businesses"**.

In the world of public speaking, there are speakers around the world who are increasingly on demand. Every conference host wants them on their stage. The invitations for me every year often gets so overwhelming that within a year, I have to turn down several hundreds of invitations to speak. When you create demand for what you do, you will become highly sought after, hence your net worth will increase.

This is also the secret of many successful companies like Coca-Cola and McDonalds. These two companies have become highly successful because they are highly sought after. In addition they are constantly looking for new ways to increase demand for their products.

From the above paragraphs, you will appreciate that it is not enough to just produce a product, you must understand ways of creating demand for your products. The more demand there is for your product and for yourself, the more your net worth.

Let's say you are creating a product right now, you need demand. Whatever you do, you must also add value to yourself in knowledge and learn how to create demand for whatever thing you are creating. You must add the value of knowledge to yourself in your area by constantly updating yourself in your field.

Attend conferences, read journals, meet the best people in your area of calling and let anyone doing better than you mentor you. That is how to become a person of worth and value. When you have the right mentors, you will have the right recommendations, the right recommendations will open up for you unbelievable doors.

Let me use this short story to illustrate for you, I hope you understand this point better because it is potent enough to change your life.

There was once a young lawyer who was struggling through the ladders of the chambers and the industry to make a name for himself. Tried as he could, he seemed to make insignificant progress and little headway. He suffered and was so confused what to do next.

After many years of struggle and little changes, he went to a very senior lawyer who was already established, renowned and a man of great reputation in the legal profession. He asked for this man's advice on what to do in order to increase his net worth and in order to become a person of value. The younger lawyer too wanted to become someone highly respected and sought after in the profession.

The senior lawyer took time to listen to the young man and said nothing, he however told him to come to his office the following day.

The following day, the old man took off his suit from the hangers, wore it, placed his hands around the young man's shoulders and walked down the street in that manner with him. When they got to the end of the street, the old lawyer would walk back with the young lawyer to another end of the street in that manner, his hands still on the young man's shoulders, his mouth all the while saying nothing. They did that for several part of that afternoon. At the end of the day, the old lawyer told the young man to go home. The young lawyer went home disappointed.

The following week, several letters began pouring into the young lawyer's office. Many people now began to demand for his services and legal advice. Letters began to pour in for him at a rate that it became overwhelming, he had to employ the assistance of more people.

Shocked, the young lawyer went to the senior lawyer to ask what the old man did that caused a drastic change in his situation. The young man noted that the old man said nothing the week before they were together.

The old man replied simply and calmly, *'That week when we walked down the street together with my arms around your shoulders, I was only recommending you to the world. The world can now trust you and your service based on my reputation'*. The young lawyer had learnt a lesson he will live to remember.

I hope you have learnt a vital lesson through that story also. Many people struggle in life because they failed to learn secrets. Progress and advancement in life however is not in the struggle, it is in the secrets that you have learnt. When you ignore the secrets and the vital principles however, a life of struggle becomes the result.

Proper mentorship can increase your demand ten-fold within the twinkling of an eye. Do not be foolish, don't ignore mentorship. However, please note that mentorship is not slavery. Mentors lay their backs for you to climb, they do not suppress you or oppress you.

CREATE A VALUE THAT HAS DEMAND

You must learn how to create demand for the service and good you are making. People who have created demand gain more net worth drastically. Even if you cannot create demand, look for demand, study and channel your effort into creating value that is already having demand. Make sure you have demand for the value you are creating.

You also have to study your competitors and find out what you can learn from them.

Study the business and look for gaps that you can fill. What is currently being done? How can you improve on what is being done? What innovations and ideas can you bring to the business? What things if done or carried out will drastically change the face of the business? These are things you should constantly ask yourself.

INCREASE YOUR NET WORTH THROUGH THE POWER OF ATTITUDE

Now we must consider other things that you can do to

improve your net worth. The next thing that will increase your net worth is the right attitude. For example, as you read from me, you have probably read in the earlier parts of the book where I said my wife does not cook. Now what a lazy mind will immediately begin to imagine is how I am so rich that I can afford such a lifestyle. A lazy mind's focus will be on my money and the superficial things rather than the essence and the wisdom behind my decision.

It is regrettable that not many people actually stop to think in life. A lot of people are just superficial with no root, hence no depth. I have major reasons why I said my wife does not cook. It is easy for you to assume that I am living well on others. Many people simply have the wrong attitude.

When you have the wrong attitude, you will not be able to think properly. Your mind will not be focused on the right things. Opportunities will pass right in front of you, but you will not be able to see them due to prejudice and the wrong attitude.

Rather than for many to learn, they are only critical. Critical people do not learn. If that is your attitude, you are always going to lose.

You are not adding worth to yourself by always being judgmental, suspicious of people and paranoid. You cannot be progressive in life that way. I personally know people who have something against everyone that exist in the world. Some people have allowed so much of bitterness and anger in their souls that they no longer see anything good in anybody or anything.

For such people, they will complain about color white being white and color black being black. And when you show them the color grey, they will complain about why it is neither black nor white. Ask yourself, are you a critical person? What kind of attitude is stopping you from learning from others? I discovered long ago that everyone can be my teacher in life and that I can learn something from everyone. When I meet a mad person, I can learn from him how not to be mad. It takes a right attitude to be able to do that. A man considered to be a man of ancient wisdom is Ralph Waldo Emerson, hear him on this quote *"In my walks, every man I meet is my superior in some way, and in that I learn from him."*

The right attitude is what creates value for you. It makes you conquer your enemies without raising a sword. It helps you learn the strategies of your enemies without being cynical or critical. It helps you make friends with people who would otherwise have been your opponents, it gives you influence and partners. It adds value to you in every sense.

These are the things that the church must teach people. The church must teach people how to have the right attitudes. The right attitude of hunger and passion, of humility, of asking questions, of seeking to add gain to oneself etc. No doubt, a man with the right attitudes will be a man of great worth. So in conclusion, if you seek to increase your worth, then you must seek to be a person with the right attitude.

INCREASE YOUR NET WORTH THROUGH THE PATH OF WISDOM

The next crucial way by which you can increase your net worth is through the path of wisdom. A path of wisdom is asking questions. Always ask questions. You may not have observed that asking questions is a significant way of adding value to yourself and increasing your net worth but it is. When you ask the right questions, you improve your chances of acquiring knowledge and getting understanding to a tricky situation.

People who ask questions are people of wisdom. Personally, I have little respect for people who talk all the time and have not perfected the art of listening and asking questions. Unless you are quiet, unless you pause and you listen, you will not acquire wisdom.

Ernest Hemingway said that, *"it takes two years to learn to speak and sixty to learn to keep quiet"*. You do not just keep quiet for nothing, you keep quiet to listen and learn.

When you keep quiet and listen, you observe. When you observe, you then ask questions on whatever may not be clear to you. How can this increase me? How can I use this to improve myself? How can I use this to improve my product? What is behind this? How can I use this to improve the lives of other people? Everything that comes to your ears must be used in asking questions. Everything that comes to your eyes must be made use of in asking questions.

You must ask questions about everything that you see and where you are right now. Questions such as, **'how can this that I am seeing help me in the fulfilment of my calling?' 'How can this help me produce a better product?' 'How can this help me produce better service?'**

Everyone around me knows they must always ask me questions. That is how I know that they are serious about learning. I once wrote a book called **'Why questions are**

more important than marriage, children and faith in God' Can you imagine that? Asking questions is more important than marriage and children and even faith in God. Of course, a lot of people might want to criticize that immediately, but there is no doubt that you will be convinced when you access the full material on the topic.

If you must increase your net worth, then you must not just know everything that has been discussed in this chapter, you must apply them also.

There is no doubt that you would have increased your net worth a great deal if you will put all of the above principles to use. I congratulate you in advance on your increasing net worth and profile.

HIGHLIGHTS
FROM CHAPTER FIVE

1. You cannot afford to be average, you cannot afford to be a mediocre, you cannot afford to be lesser than anything that God has made you, hence you must seek to always increase your net worth on the earth.

2. Your net worth and the value you produce in an hour directly depends on how much value you have earlier added to yourself.

3. The amount of value you have added to your mind is what determines what comes out of you.

4. It is almost impossible to see any truly successful person who is not a reader. You cannot see anyone who truly made it to the top who is not addicted to books or to reading.

5. The quality of your labor also decides your net worth. The world will pay anything and any amount to a man who can not only do his job well, but who can do his job excellently well.

6. To a person of quality, there is really no small thing. There is absolutely nothing small. Excellence is in the details, in the minutest of things.

7. A major way your value and net worth is estimated is by the demand for you and your product and services.

CHAPTER 6
....

EXPANDING YOUR NET WORTH

Many ideas and strategies have already been discussed in increasing your net worth. There are still so much more tips and strategies which you can use to increase, grow and expand your net worth.

In this chapter, I will be giving certain rare tools to grow and expand your net worth.

Remember that I said earlier that increasing your net worth is your personal responsibility. It is not just enough to create your net worth. You must ensure that your net worth and profile is constantly on the increase.

There have been many stories of people who at a point in their life were people of influence and great net worth, yet ended their lives in penury and great shame. What could have caused that? The reason is because after such people created their net worth, they failed to apply strategies, ideas and principles that will constantly grow and expand that net worth.

So how can you grow, increase and expand your net worth?

EXPAND YOUR NET WORTH
THROUGH THE POWER OF FOCUS

A way by which you can expand and increase your net worth is through the power of focus. This is one of my favorite topics to discuss with people. It is my favorite because the power of focus has caused me to win on many grounds in my life.

A lot of people who know me personally understand this to be one of my secrets and a principle which gives me one of my greatest leverages.

I implore you my dear reader to pay attention to this that I am about to discuss with you. As a matter of fact and without any doubt, if you pay attention to this singular point alone, you would have increased your own net worth many folds.

The ability to work and not notice anything else. The ability to focus and concentrate, the ability to give the maximum and optimal attention to what you are doing increases your output at least three times. Again, that depends on your level of concentration. That depends on your level of focus, your concentration could increase you from three times to ten times.

Focus, just like I discussed with you much earlier in the book is giving all your senses to the task at hand. In an earlier illustration, we talked of the light and the lamp, let us bring back that illustration again.

A light that is not focused cannot cut through anything, but when it is focused through a laser, it becomes fire. A light that is focused can cut through a tree, wall, metal or iron. A focused light can cut through anything and any barriers.

Focus increases your efficiency many times over. The ability to convert one hour of your day and bring yourself to focus, working very hard on same thing, will make you get results that will amaze you.

Many examples abound in this area. Let me share

one of them with you. Have you heard of a man called George Washington Carver? He was a scientist and a discoverer. As a matter of fact, his discoveries using just the peanut saved an entire nation from economic recession. From the peanut alone, he was able to make up to three hundred to four hundred amazing discoveries. What was the secret of this man; Focus.

From written accounts of his life, we are told that this scientist will get into his laboratory on Monday morning and often will not get out of the laboratory until Friday evening, surviving on drinking just water. As a matter of fact, he does not get out of the laboratory willingly on Friday, it is his aides and workers who would usually break down the door after knocking repeatedly with no response. The man was always so focused on working on his project that he was totally oblivious of any distractions around him. When eventually they accessed him, he would ask why they were calling him out of the lab so early that he just got in on his projects that morning. His workers out of shock would then respond that it is Friday, not Monday.

The man was so focused that he couldn't even observe he had been working for a week and not a day. There is no way such a man with such level of concentration will not be a genius. There is no way such a way with such laser focus of attention on his job will not be the best at what he does, a man of immense worth and value. Can you give same level of attention and concentration to what you currently do? Can you be found in solitude for an entire week working away to solve a problem? Can you become a person of focus on what you do?

When I learnt this secret, I began to take entire week

out of the whole month away on personal solitude away from every distraction around me. It is extremely difficult if not impossible to be a person of worth without such a lifestyle.

Why is it that people like George Washington Carver who would go into a laboratory on a Monday would often be gone for a week till Friday, not eating and in that enclosure doing research? He understood the principle of focus as a way of increasing his worth and value.

Another example is that of autistic patients and savants. A savant is a person affected with a disability (such as autism or mental retardation) who exhibits exceptional skill or brilliance in some limited field such as music, mathematics or painting.

A popular example of a savant is Kim Peek, often called the 'rain man' who has read over 12,000 books and remembers every single thing he has read. Why am I bringing up this story and example, because it has been found that the reason autistic patients and savants possess such incredible ability and genius is due to their depth of focus and concentration.

Autistic patients are often not interested about so many things going on around them, hence they have the ability to focus on a specified thing and become the perfect master of that thing. It often seems that whatever this special people focus on, they tend to become a genius at it.

While the goal of the story is not to despise those who are autistic, it is to help you see the incredible power latent within every one of us if only we will put a fraction of our concentration power to use.

So again, what was the secret of George Washington

Carver? It was focus, and that was why he became one of the greatest inventors in the world.

Well, there is no doubt that if you will implement all these that you have learnt, you will become a person of tremendous worth and value. However, another way by which you can increase your self-worth is through the instrumentality of diligence.

EXPAND YOUR NET WORTH
THROUGH DILIGENCE

Diligence is a virtue that you must master if you will expand and increase your net worth.

Diligence is doing everything to the best of your knowledge. Diligence is being concerned with everything and not just what you think pertains to you alone.

A lot of people dodge responsibilities and behave in a way that nothing concerns them. Nothing is ever their responsibility and nothing concerns them. They care about nothing.

If you must increase your net worth however, you must understand that everything concerns you. Everything concerns a diligent person and a diligent person is concerned by everything.

A diligent person is interested in everything. A diligent person takes interest in how everything is done. He takes careful note especially of the things that will help him to become better in his area of calling.

I have often wondered why people attend conferences and programs and refuse to take notes or write anything down. Some attend lectures and come back empty handed. The reason is simple, they are not diligent. They are not interested. Though they are in class with their eyes physically open, their minds are not. Therefore, the first key to being diligent is having interest in what you do. When you are interested in your work and assignment, you will give all of your heart and attention to it. You will pay careful attention to every detail.

YOUR LIFE DEPENDS ON THE
VALUE YOU CREATE IN AN HOUR

Let me give you some examples of how your life depends on the value you are able to create in an hour of your day.

You could use time to become anything you want to become. There is no limit, you have the wealth of time. I have often emphasized that the wealth of time makes everyone equally rich in life. When a man who currently has no job on his hands understands this secret, he will see why he is probably wealthier than anybody else around him. That though is a discussion for another book.

Thanks to the wealth of time, you can become anything that you wish to become. It all depends on how you use your time. With time you can become an engineer, a medical doctor, a pharmacist, a writer, a journalist, a singer.

Are you wasting your time? Are you spending your time or investing and converting your time into added value. In life, it is either you are adding value to yourself or you are adding value to others. We already established that before in this book. It is either you are paying attention to details or you are glossing over everything, wasting your own life. You can determine from now not to waste your time, you can determine not to waste your life. You can determine to become a person of value by discovering your calling and working very hard to develop yourself. You can become a person of focus and diligence. You can build a prison around yourself so that your time and life will not be wasted. If you do not build a prison around yourself and guard your time jealously, others will put you in their own prison and waste your time immensely. At the end of your life, you would have lived a pitiable life, you would have ended up wasting yourself in the business of others with no value to yourself, to your family, to your generation and to your world.

Again, understand that diligence will improve you. Diligence to everything that has been shared with you. Diligence to your calling, diligence to improving yourself by asking questions, diligence to the right and solid mentorship, diligence to doing everything that will increase your net worth.

It will be good to remind you that diligence also is paying attention to details. These are the right ways for you to use your time.

Add value to the products
you create

Another way we establish that you can increase your self-worth is by adding value not just to yourself and to others, but also to the products that you create. Few add value to themselves but extremely few add value to a product that they are creating. You could use your time to create some valuable products to the world.

That's how you create a value chain and that is how you can become anything you want.

An example is a book I read a long while ago where

someone talked about how to become a millionaire. When I read the book, I discovered that the reason why I was not yet a millionaire up till that time was because I had spent all my time in church, and all my time in events. I was a busy Pastor and I hardly had time for anything else.

Right there I knew if I would give two years to study on the laws of money, I knew I would become a millionaire. I achieved the goal in 9 months. You have not paid the currency of time required to achieve a thing that is why you have not achieved it yet.

Another example that will help you to understand better is this and I hope you understand this well. I used to be just a pastor before, but then I knew I was not just interested in people coming to church for religious activities, and the country is unchanged. I discovered that I was more interested in changing countries and the whole of societies.

I knew if I wanted to become an expert in national transformation and an expert in changing nations, I needed to give my life to studying that. So I invested about ten years of my life studying principles of how to change nations and bring about national transformation.

I'm not sure how many experts you know in turning around countries and entire nations like I have done from the pulpit. My whole church is centered on turning around nations and bringing about transformations. All my members are trained for this purpose.

When I talk now about politics, economy etc people are amazed. It is because I have devoted time to create value in myself on how to change a nation. I became a millionaire in nine months. I became a national transformer in 8 years because I gave my life to becoming an expert in those areas.

Now, with the instrumentality of this book, I am discussing time with you. I do not know if you have read books on time management, everyone seem to be writing and talking about time management same way. I decided that my approach to all things will be different, same with this topic I am discussing with you right now. Often you will not read on time management like you have read in this book. People who discuss on this topic often repeat each other because they read same books and access same sources.

But through the power of focus and the tool of diligence, I dug deep not just into the Bible, but into the knowledge of the world and the wisdom of God. I dug deep into God in personal relationship with him.

I have been able to write whole books on time and time management focused on transforming entire nations. I am proving to people that the governments of developing nations, especially a nation like my dear country Nigeria is in crisis due to one major thing. The abuse and total disregard for time.

When developing nations pay attention to developing their worth, especially by paying attention to private and corporate time, these nations can double or triple her economy. An example of a nation that can achieve this is Nigeria. We can sit together right now were it to be possible and I will give you mathematical proofs that Nigeria can triple her economy through the understanding of time.

Developing nations and especially the whole continent of Africa can take hold of this one insight and turn around entire societies, and that is even without selling anything yet, just entirely through the power of time.

Pay attention to time

Time is so powerful, nations are rich because of their understanding and conversion of time. Also nations are poor because they fail to understand time.

Understanding of time will turn around entire nations. You can use this knowledge to add value to yourself. Time can be converted to double the GDP of a country. Right now the GDP of Nigeria is 500 billion dollars.

There is a book already on how Nigeria can double her GDP to become One trillion(dollars) within a year.

You can use time to transform anything. You can use time to become anything also. If there is anything you do not have now, it is because you have not dedicated the time and have not converted enough time to have it. You have not bought that specific thing through the currency of time.

I have proved this principle first in my own life before I teach them. How have I done some of these things? I have a disciple who is a professor of Chemistry in Atlanta Georgia.

He lived in America for about 30 years, teaching Chemistry and Physics. Now, on a particular encounter, what he said to me was one of the greatest compliments I have received. This gentleman told me he never understood God's perspective of mathematics until he met me.

Now understand this, I grew up in a village, I graduated from a school in the village that had no Mathematics teacher. I passed Mathematics only by hard work and self-study. I was not a science student neither did I study physics. There was even no physics as a subject in my school. I never saw a laboratory in my whole life till I came to Europe. We never had chemistry as a subject. But I created time to add value to myself. I created time to study deeply into all of these interest areas.

This professor of science said that he understood biblical insight of physics and chemistry only when he met me. Those were the subject he lectures on. He's a professor. He also added this within the compliments he gave to me, he said, *"I never knew Physics, Mathematics and Chemistry were in the Bible until I met you".* What a regard.

Those were not my words, those were the words of a knowledgeable person. When I saw what Mark Zuckerberg did as young man, a little above the age of 20, I challenged myself. I again applied the principle of knowing that I could become anything, the principle of knowing that I could bring solutions and answers to any problem in the world. I began to challenge myself on inventions. Now, the things I have done in these areas will amuse you.

With the right use of time, you can solve any problem in the world

Yes, can you believe that? Can you believe that you can solve any problem in the world, all that you need is the right understanding and use of time. We could bring solutions and answers to anything and any problem in the world.

There was a man called Malcolm Gladwell who invented the 10,000 hour principle of developing a skill.

What Malcolm said was that it takes approximately 10,000 hours to become a world-class expert on any skill. If you must become a near-genius, if you must become a person with a sharp skill, capable of developing solutions to pressing problems, then you must have practiced a single skill for at least ten thousand hours.

"I fear not the man who has practiced 10,000 kicks once, but I fear the man who had practiced one kick 10,000 times." (Bruce Lee)

You can just convert your time like Malcolm Gladwell said into a world class skill.

If you will dedicate at least 10, 000 hours into anything, you can become anything or discover anything. If you will dedicate ten thousand hours into a particular line of research, into practicing the piano, into learning to dance, into clothe and fashion designing, you will be able to solve lots of problems within a specified area with your unique skill.

When I saw what Mark Zuckerberg had done, I knew I had a secret and that I could apply it. I told myself, "If a young man and a man with no access to the wisdom of God, someone who has no personal relationship with God could come up with Microsoft, Internet, Google, etc I decided to dedicate myself into research.

The result was that I came up with a concept, a unique concept, it is an Internet concept. We submitted this concept to Silicon Valley and experts who work with Steve Jobs and Mark Zuckerberg said our invention will be better than what Facebook and Google have done. The idea is revolutionary and it will revolutionize the world. This project is being developed and will be patented soon.

I have more, I've got more desires in my soul. I want to come up with an invention that will make all men to hear the gospel. I want an invention that would have 5 billion people on a platform.

A design to actualize this is what I have done. This invention will bring together 5 billion people, it's been critiqued by silicon valley and they attest to it being extra ordinary.

This is just an idea. I am not a science person but through self-education and conversion of time to add value to myself, I was able to create an invention. I have been told this invention is greater than Facebook.

That is what you can do, this is what all men can do because we all possess that invisible energy, that force, that god-like nature within us. It is present in every one of us and within every single human being without any exceptions.

If you are African and you are reading this, you can devote yourself to finding answers to energy problem or to problems of electricity and you will find answers to it. You can do anything that you devote your time to do, you can become anything that you devote your time to become. You can become anything, it is your choice.

I want to bring enlightenment to all men especially to Christians to become enlightened. I want to bring light to people's minds. Everything is possible if you learn how to convert time. You can bring solution to the problem of diseases in Africa and the plague of poverty in the world. You can convert time into anything that you want to become in this life.

I have another illustration here and this will perhaps be the last in this chapter. I came up with a technology and idea of creating the greatest business ideas in the world.

Only scientists and learned men, men of skill will understand this. I once discussed this with a friend, a professor. He confessed it was huge and that he could not even handle it.

To handle such an idea, only scientists will work on the project. This will be a tool for Africa and I am convinced about the revolution it will bring to the continent that was otherwise termed the Dark Continent. When ideas like this are up and running within the continent, no one will dare call us illiterate and backward any longer.

We will gather the best of scientists in Africa. I will reveal and teach this to them and train them on how to create the business ideas in the world in the area of food production. I have this right now. I am sharing all of this with you so that you too can know that you can discover whatever it is that you want to discover, you can be an answer to a problem, you can be the miracle the world needs in the areas of cancer, HIV/AIDS, diabetes etc. You can solve named and unnamed diseases with no current cure. You can be the solution.

With all these that have been said and discussed, I quite understand the ignorance of people when they tell me, *"Pastor, face your calling and just preach"*. Why should you limit God when God has given you the mind of Christ? Why should I limit God when I know the secret of conversion and that I can become anything that I want to become in life?

Again, let me reinstate that you too can become anything you want to become in life. You have the greatest wealth that is available on earth, the wealth of time, if you will use the force of conversion through labor, through work, you can choose what you want to become and do conversion on it. Use the principles you have learnt in this book to achieve it. You can become anything.

THERE IS NO EXCUSE FOR FAILURE IN LIFE

Everyone knows this already, when I became a millionaire in 9 months, I decided to create other millionaires. Within 3 years, we had created more than 200 other millionaires, all of them are alive and testifying. Why? Because life is about the secrets you know. Life is really buried in the secrets.

Here is one more principle for you to know, understand and apply. Read this carefully, I hope you understand it quite well. There is no excuse for failure in life. What you just read right now is so important I need to repeat it for you in bold letters, there is no excuse for failure in life. There is no failure in life either. There should be no one who fails in life. No one should fail. There is no room for failing. There is no reason why you should fail.

Why do people fail nevertheless? Though I am too convinced there is no reason why people should fail and not become successful. Still people fail. Are you still wondering why?

It's simple and here is the reason, because they do not know the laws and the secrets of life. This is why I have devoted my life to teaching laws and principles.

If you attend Churches regularly on Sundays, then you have Sundays to listen to sermons but you need a hungry search for laws and principles. Life is about secrets, about principles, about laws. The laws and principles of life are what make life predictable. Yes, the laws and principles that govern life make it predictable. Hence all you need is to understand what these laws and principles are and apply them. This book is entirely about some of those laws and principles.

Let me tell you this, the only people who fail are those who fail because they do not know the secrets of success. Otherwise, there are those who know but are not willing to pay the price of hard work or conversion.

There are no failures and no reason to fail in life. No one was created a failure. The only people who fail, do so because they do not know the secrets and the laws of life, the principle of success or maybe they know but are negligent of the demands of success. Again, life is predictable.

In all my books and teachings, I emphasize on the laws and principles that govern life, hence you have an opportunity to learn.

Again, life is predictable. Life is built on laws. Life is built on certain laws, hence such laws make life foreseeable. That is why people who do not know God can be successful.

I am about to tell you something that will shake you up a bit so I advise that you brace up and get ready for it. People are often shocked when I say to them that *"On the earth, you do not need to know God to be successful"*. I guess you are shocked now. I told you you'd be shocked. Let me repeat it again carefully and I want you to read it carefully, *"On the earth, you do not need to know God to be successful"* If you will like to argue with that, then the Forbes list of the world's richest men is there for you to look at. There is no Christian among the names on the top of the list. God did not design that Christians should be excluded from the list, the ignorance of Christians did.

On this earth, you only need to know the laws of God and the principles he has established to operate on earth for your success. If you know these laws, you obey and apply them, you will be successful. If you do not obey these laws, you will be poor, wretched and unattractive even though you are the most praying human being on the earth.

You do not need to be a believer or go to church, you just need to believe in God's laws and to believe in yourself.

However, I must state that if you do not believe in God, you will still go to hell despite the fact that you are successful.

If we believe in God, then why don't we use his principles and laws? Because we don't use the principles and laws of God is why we are not successful. We do not obey his laws.

We only believe in God and not his laws and principles that is why it seems God does not help us anymore. You must now understand his laws. You must understand his principles, the way he makes everything to function.

When you exploit his laws and his principles, when you submit yourself to his rules, then you know you can become anything you want to become. One of such laws is the law of the conversion of time which we have discussed the whole while. We can find solution to any problem. We can resolve any issue if we will dedicate our time into finding solutions and answers to problems.

You and I can begin finding answers to the equations of life. We can choose to dedicate ourselves, in spite of obstacles to put any target before us and we will attain it.

If any human being was able to attain any amount of success or any achievement in any sphere of life, then anyone can repeat that success. If anyone was able to achieve anything, then you too can do same and do better.

Your success however is only dependent on one thing, you have to discover the secrets. You also have to be willing to pay the price. I told you earlier of designing an invention which experts have said is better than Facebook, better than what Zuckerberg had done. It was extremely challenging for me. Mark developed Facebook in perhaps 6 years, I spent two years of my life researching and developing what could bring the entire world into same platform. In two years, I got the solution. I got the illumination and design. Something that could communicate the gospel to everyone even in the remotest areas.

Well I hope you have learnt a lesson or two on how to increase your net worth. I hope your life will now be for the better. I hope our world will feel your impact. I hope you can use these vital lessons to become a person of value.

Don't just be religious, do not kill time through religiosity, account for your life. Time is life.

HIGHLIGHTS
FROM CHAPTER SIX

1. The ability to focus and concentrate, the ability to give the maximum and optimal attention to what you are doing increases your output at least three times.

2. The ability to convert one hour of your day and bring yourself to focus, working very hard on same thing, will make you get results that will amaze you.

3. If you must increase your net worth, you must understand that everything concerns you. Everything concerns a diligent person and a diligent person is concerned by everything.

4. You could use time to become anything you want to become on the earth.

5. When developing nations pay attention to developing their worth, especially by paying attention to private and corporate time, these nations can double or triple their economy.

6. You can solve any problem in the world, all that you need is the right understanding and use of time.

7. There is no excuse for failure in life.

CHAPTER 7

·······························

HOW TO DETERMINE YOUR NET WORTH

Do you know you can determine your own net worth on the earth? Do you know you can set your mind on what value you want to have in a few years, and with planning you can achieve it?

Right now, I want to teach you how you can determine your own net worth. In this chapter, we will also be considering critically how to increase your net worth using the currency of time.

The essence of this book is creating your net worth. Earlier we have talked about how to increase our net worth. We have also considered in details what a man's net worth is. We have come to understand the difference between a man's worth and his net worth. A man's worth does not depend on anything he possesses but a man's net worth depends on the values he has created within himself and the value that he carries.

In this chapter however, we will be considering something highly critical and different. The point of consideration here is totally different. The topic or point of focus we have to consider in the next few pages is how to create your net worth, net worth is totally different from worth.

I must emphasize that many times, people are confused about the difference between worth and net worth. I have made this clarification for you, you have to always remember and understand the difference between the two.

First you must understand that every man has a basic worth. We all have a worth and we deserve something because we are carrying the image of God, we are created in the image and likeness of God. That is the basic worth that every man possesses and carries.

However, when we talk about net worth, we are getting on to a totally different ball game. So, the focus for us right now is creating your net worth through your time currency.

EVERY MAN HAS A WORTH BUT NOT EVERY MAN HAS A NET WORTH

Every man has a worth but not every man has a net worth. To put it more accurately, every man was given a basic worth or capital to begin life with. And like all issues of life, every man trades differently with his capital. Some have traded with this capital and have made lot of increase with it. Unfortunately, we have a greater percentage of people in the world who are not even aware of this capital, talk less of trading with it. This basic capital is the capital of time.

If you read the previous chapters carefully, you will understand that everyman on earth is equally wealthy because every man on earth has equal time each day. The difference between people all over the world is that men trade with their time differently. While there are a lot of people who do not value time and are not living and using their time consciously, there are a few others in the world who are conscious and are trading with their time judiciously.

Earlier, we discussed quite well about time and considered all the aspects that have to do with time. If you read those chapters carefully, you will understand by now that you are equally as wealthy as any other man on this planet.

Everyone is wealthy and we are all equally gifted by God almighty. God gave to each man every day an equal amount of wealth. God gives us the riches of time on a daily basis. He endows us from heaven on daily basis. What we do with that wealth or resource that we are given on daily basis is every man's choice.

That choice however is what separates our individual net worth and value through life. God on his own side has done what He needs to do. Unfortunately, many so called learned and educated people are still busy going to places of worship and religious centres to beg God to give them something that he has already given them. People pray all kinds of ridiculous prayers. I am embarrassed personally when I hear people pray prayers such as *"Oh God bless me, bless my work, bless this, do this"*. What depth of ignorance.

We are just wasting our time and troubling God for nothing. God must be looking down upon us with such pity. Yet there is nothing that he can do except we pay the sacrifice and the personal price of acquiring knowledge.

God has given us many different resources. In fact, everything that exists within you and around you right now is a resource which can be used and converted to produce whatever it is that you want.

For example, God has given you your eyes, nose, ears, hands etcetera. Some people come to this world without eyes or legs, some people even came without hands. But you have everything, so you are already endowed by God.

OUR BIGGEST ENDOWMENT IS TIME

The biggest and most important endowment that we all have is the endowment of time. That wealth is given to everybody equally and it's being renewed to us on daily basis.

A part of the scriptures says that the faithfulness of God is renewed every morning. God is equally faithful to every man and that faithfulness is expressed as his laws and principles which he established upon the earth. One of the strongest guiding principles on the earth is the principle of time.

So we are all wealthy, we are all rich, but what you do with that endowment; what you do with that daily wealth is entirely up to you.

The key to realizing and to maximizing this vast amount of wealth that you have got is called conversion. Earlier, we considered conversion and what you can do with the wealth of your time. We discussed already about the most important things you can do with your time.

The most important instrument with which you convert your time is the instrument of work. If you must convert your time, then you must work. Without understanding the principle of work and how to use work to convert your time into the right products, you will end up wasting your wealth every day. You will end up squandering all that you have and all that you've got, you will end up wasting your life.

Without work there will be no blessing. Work brings out the potential in you. Work beautifies you. Work moves you towards your purpose daily. Work helps you maximize your brain and helps you to think. When you have not discovered the beauty of work, you are only surviving, you are not yet existing. You are everyday being laid up as a material for other people to make use of. Without work, there is no production and effective management of your life. With work, you become a solution to the problem of the world and the problem of everyone around you. To put it in simple terms, without work, you have no value. Men who do not work constitute a waste.

(When I'm talking about work, I'm not talking about job)

I am going to discuss this with you in greater details in the next chapter. I am going to show you why you must instantly become a workaholic. However, right now we are focused on learning how to create your net worth through your time currency.

Net worth is not talking about your worth as a human being. Rather, net worth is talking about how much you cost, how much you are valuable to the people around you and how valuable you are in the market place.

Net worth is talking about how valuable you are in the eyes of men, in the eyes of the world, in the eyes of people. Your net worth describes how people see you, how much people are willing to offer for you or your products to be around them. The real world we live in estimates every human on earth not by their worth, but by their net worth.

You may not like it but that is just the real world we live in. Your net worth depends on how much value you have been able to create in yourself. For example, I have a couple of young people who work around me. Some work on my social media platforms and others have varied assignments they do for me.

Some of these people edit my books and for that I pay them a certain amount of money. Now why is that I'm not paying just any person or someone who is just passing by that amount of money? Why am I not just giving money to just anybody?

The reason is quite simple; because the people who work with me have created value in themselves. Somebody could say that I pay too much money to these young people, someone might complain that the remuneration is too high seeing that many of them are young and students, well another person might just say it's okay.

Whatever it is, I am not just paying for the work that you do, I am paying for the amount of value that you have successfully created within yourself.

Let's say I pay you a thousand dollars for an assignment that you complete for me. Someone who is merely observing may question the amount you are paid, there are people who will look down on what you do and complain, making it look like you didn't do anything. There are some others who will boast that they can also do what you do, even though they lack the same skill with which you did the job. Everyone thinks they can accomplish same task that a skillful person has done because he made it look so effortless.

Have you ever watched soccer players on the field of play? How many times have you made boasts that you can also score goals if put on the field of play? Many people also complain about how much boxers and heavy weight champions are paid for their titles. If it were allowed, a lot of people would jump into the boxing ring for the sake of money, only forgetting it might be a jump to their last fight. An untrained person who jumps into the ring for the sake of money won't survive to tell the tale.

What am I trying to point out? What the boxers and heavy weight champions are being paid for, what soccer players are being paid, what Olympic champions are being paid for? It is not just about the entertainment that they provide, it is the value that they have created within themselves. It is how high they have improved on their skills and how rare it is to find someone else who can do what they do the way they do it.

I could do that, you may say but wait till you try it out. Why it might be impossible for you to recreate same intrigue, same interest and same charm that any celebrity out there possesses right now is because you have not created same value that such celebrity has created within himself in yourself. I hope you understand this quite well now.

Well, there are so many people who make attempts with different work around me and simply fail. They fail to do a satisfactory job. You will agree with me that it is simply impossible to pay those who cannot create very standard work same money as those who create excellent work for obvious reasons. Because I couldn't see the value of their work, they do not get appreciated with same value. The value of the work of such people is not convincing to me that they have what it takes.

So what made those who create excellent work to convince me that they have what it takes? Because these people have taken time to add value to themselves. The people who work to edit my books have developed themselves in the skill of language and the skill of writing. Some have added value to themselves in the area of knowledge and some among them are simply highly skilled with their hands.

When these people convert some amount of time in their lives to develop that skill, then they get appreciated. Maybe you spent 1000 hours in school writing and learning how to write, some of these my dear friends have spent more than five thousand hours writing, developing and sharpening that skill. Perhaps while their colleagues busied themselves with many intangible thoughts and duties, they busied themselves focusing on their gift and working way into the night to sharpen their gifts, adding value to themselves.

A man called Henry Wadsworth Longfellow once said that *"The heights that great men reached and kept were not attained by sudden flight, but they, while their companions slept, were toiling upward in the night"*. I really do hope you understand this point that we are raising and sharing about here. This is really potent enough to change your life.

Right now, you can spot the difference when my staff write or speak. You cannot argue the fact that they are highly trained. I have poured myself into them every night and day and you can see a bit of me in every one of them. They also have taken the time to get trained. They have taken the time to toil and become sharp, distinct and well defined. Each of them holds a ground, a field, an area of calling that they dominate effectively.

Thanks to time, thanks to the value of time, these fellows converted their time into value, they converted their time into worth. They endured the pain and they created that value within themselves.

They didn't just allow time to pass by even though the period of training is the period of suffering. Everyone suffers through the period of creating value within themselves. These my dear friends were no exception at all. They suffered too, they laboured, they toiled. A lot of them went through difficult times at the time they were creating that value within themselves, some of them probably had nothing to eat.

The Process of adding value to yourself could be Painful

When you are in the process of adding value to yourself, nobody sees the product yet, nobody sees the result yet. Nobody sees the product at the time because you were in a process. And if there is anything that process does well, it is that process masks the product. Process usually does not reveal the product until the end.

Let me give you an example and illustration. Have you ever been to a building site before? Have you ever been to an estate that is under construction? What do you see on these sites? You see rubble, you see dirt. There is nothing attractive to you about the estate because it is under construction.

Well, it is like that because the estate is under process, process has hidden the beauty of what is being built. You cannot see it but within a space of time an edifice will emerge. It is almost unbelievable when you visit that same site again within a few months later. Your mouth would probably be opened in wonder at what will be staring at you. Same it is when you are building yourself and adding value to yourself.

The process of adding value to yourself is extremely painful, especially at the initial stages. Your body will be giving you all manner of suggestions and will give you reasons while that personal discipline you have chosen is impossible. When you start training yourself, few hours will begin to seem like days and days will begin to seem like decades. But if you can stick to your training, if you can keep adding value to yourself, no doubt about it, within a short time, you will become a champion, the whole world will hear about you soon.

When I resumed at my school in Russia, I applied this same principle. Because I resumed to school very late from Nigeria, one of my professors told me point blank that it would be impossible for me to cope academically. In fact he was so sure that he swore as an atheist to go light candles in Church if I ever passed. I knew the solution was for me to add value to myself, I needed to develop myself aggressively, I needed to put knowledge into my brain.

One of the decisions I immediately took was to spend six hours every single day in the library including Saturdays and Sundays. I determined that there was nothing that was going to make me break from that discipline.

Was it easy? Of course no. Was it difficult? Saying it was difficult will be an understatement. As a matter of fact, when I had spent an hour in the initial days when I began, it often seemed I had spent the entire six hours. I would sit down for a few minutes and would instantly begin to imagine the clock running faster and the day getting dark. It was tough but young as I was, I was a man of resolve. I stuck to the discipline.

What was the result of the exercise? I did not just pass, I excelled above everyone who had been in those classes before me. I passed the Russian language more than the Russian kids who were born and bred in their own native land. I kept adding value to myself same way till I left the school. Eventually, I was able to set an academic record that remained unbeaten for more than twenty five years, even after I had left the University. That is how to become a person of worth and value. That is how to create your net worth. I understood that I could convert my time into value and if I generated great worth of value, I would be a person of immense worth.

YOU CAN BE A PERSON OF WORTH

My dear friend, you can be a person of worth and value. You can achieve far more than you think is possible. You can do the impossible. You can become a person of immense worth. You can create value to yourself and for your world. Through the value that you have created within yourself, you can solve any problem in this world.

I am fond of saying to people that every problem in this world is only making a demand or request for someone with a commensurate amount of value. What am I saying and talking about? The problem of Cancer in this world is only making a demand on someone who has created enough value within himself to solve that problem. The problem of electricity within your country is only making a request for anyone who has developed himself up to the extent of solving that problem. The problem of the economy, of commerce and industry is not actually the problem, the main problem is that there is no one who has created enough value within himself to be a solution to each of those challenges.

Now that you know this, what will you do? What problem will you solve? What solution will you become? What chosen field will you decide to start creating wealth within yourself for?

WHAT IS TIME MAKING OUT OF YOU? WHAT ARE YOU MAKING OUT OF TIME?

You must believe in your activity, you must believe in what you are doing, you must also believe in what you can do. You must believe in the process, you must have faith in what you are becoming, you must have faith in the future product you are going to give.

Many of the people who work for me and who are staff on my team were once students. Indeed, every one of us was once a student and in school. But beyond what you are being thought in school, what are you teaching yourself to become?

There is that which the school is making you and there is that which you can make of yourself. A lot of people pay the school to become one thing or the other, actually what you are paying the school for is the process and the discipline they will instil in you to become what you want to become. Beyond that however, you have to reach deep within yourself and offer more than the school can ever make demand of you.

If you are a young person reading this, I sincerely hope that you will not waste your life. I sincerely hope that you will not just go through school and endure your days while in school. I sincerely hope that you will become conscious of your environment and the process of what you are going through. I sincerely hope that you will lay demands upon your life, and put yourself within the process of what you want to become.

Earlier, I was sharing with you how some of the people who were working for me began working for me when they were students. Each of them perhaps had a personal challenge, many were stranded and without money. Of course, students are always looking for ways to get more money.

Before this young people began working for me, nobody was paying them the amount and kind of money I was paying them for their work. So, young as they were, they were using their whole life to develop themselves. They kept developing themselves in the hope that their pay day was coming. Eventually, when some of them met me and I told them how much I was going to pay them for their work, they just could not believe it. Many still did not believe till they got paid the actual money.

ENDURE THE PAINFUL PROCESS OF ADDING VALUE TO YOURSELF

When you are converting time to add value to your-self, it could seem like a wasted time. It could seem like you are punishing yourself. It could seem like you are anti-social and ignorant.

Now read this carefully, whatever amount of time that you convert to add value to yourself is never a wasted time. Time is never wasted if you are using it to add value to yourself.

Note this again, time is never a wasted time when that time is being converted to add value to others.

Here is the kicker, though you might not see the result immediately but when you are adding value to yourself, you are on an upward match in life. When you know the quality of time you are using to add value to yourself, then you know the quality of value you can add to others and to your world.

When you know of the quality of conversion you are doing to add value to yourself, that time is never wasted. Such time is invested.

When you are adding value to others, you are also in a great way investing your time. Converting your time to add value to others as well is never wasted. You have a greater leverage and a better reward especially if those people you are investing your time in are responsible and accountable people.

If you teach them responsibility, if you teach them how to go and practice what you've given to them, that time is an invested time.

So when you are adding value to yourself or when you are adding value to others, it becomes a way by which you are multiplying yourself and getting multiple results for what you do. It means many people can now do what you alone have been doing, it means there are many more like you on the surface of the earth multiplying and duplicating your effort.

Let us back track a bit to the discussion on hand. When you are converting your time to add value to yourself, that conversion process adding value to you is called creating net worth. You are thereby creating your net worth. Do you understand that?

Maybe it will take you a few years or upwards of five thousand hours to create your net worth. It may take you several years to keep on adding value to yourself concerning that particular thing you have chosen to improve yourself upon.

Perhaps it costs you several hours, perhaps it takes you just eight hours, whatever amount of time it takes you, you have to keep on working. Many people who quit in life quit at the stage of training. Many people left their preparation grounds and turned their backs on their calling. I have always been quite impressed with how soccer players train in all seasons in preparation for their big games. Even when there is no game coming up, they still have to keep training to keep their body in form and shape. They train when it is snowing and they train when it is raining. That must be the condition for you if you must win in life.

There may not be any immediate competition, there may not be any big game coming up for you, there may not be a significant event where you have been invited to, but if you must create your net worth and be a person with a great net worth, then you must keep training.

Several years ago, one of my friends who owns a big Church in the United States and who often gives out his church hall for concerts and programs told me something very important. He said when the church hall is given out to rent for concerts, preparations for the concert would have begun weeks before by the celebrities and the performers who were going to have the concert.

According to him, many times these people were training and preparing up to fifteen hours every day for a period of about two weeks for a concert which was probably going to last two or three hours. Now that is how you win in life, that is how you create your net worth, that is how you force your world to look up to you with respect. When you see a man who is putting forth such amount of diligence into his work, it is only a matter of time before such a person becomes a super star and one that the entire world cannot do without.

When you are adding value to yourself within a period, it is most likely that you do not have a physical product yet to show for it, probably you don't produce services yet. Maybe that value you are adding to yourself has not become visible yet, but if you know what you are doing and you believe in the quality of value that you are forming in yourself, then you keep training, training, training.

IF YOU CAN ENDURE THE PROCESS, YOUR PAY DAY IS COMING

The value you have created will later work for you. The value you have created in yourself will later run returns to you. That value you have created and formed within yourself will advertise you, it will showcase you to the world. The value you have created will later on pay you for the rest of your life. That value you have created and formed within yourself will yield returns for you and bring wealth to you. That value, the immense wealth within you will attract whatever your need in life might be. If you will keep working hard, your pay day is coming.

Now pay attention to this, I know you are probably working very hard on yourself right now and you are probably about to quit because you have not seen results yet. You probably want to stop all preparations you have been in yourself because you have long expected glory-day and it has not come, if you will pay attention to this, it will change your life forever.

Those little hours that you are right now using in adding value to yourself will become your bread tomorrow, it will become your finances tomorrow, it will become your greatness tomorrow, it will become your net worth tomorrow, the value that you have added to yourself decides your net worth tomorrow.

I have learnt that value creation is cumulative. What do I mean? The little preparations you made on yourself today will add up to the little preparations you will make on yourself tomorrow, if you will keep at it and will not stop, eventually all the little preparations will add up to produce from you a star, a glorified personality. Do you doubt what I said about your preparation being cumulative? Let me tell you the story of the Chinese bamboo tree.

In China, there is a tree that has been called the Chinese bamboo tree. I think it is an ancient story and one that is capable of impacting you greatly. This remarkable tree is different from most trees in that it doesn't grow in the usual fashion. While most trees grow steadily over a period of years, the Chinese bamboo tree doesn't break through the ground for the first four years. Then, in the fifth year, a remarkable thing begins to happen – the tree begins to grow at a rate that is totally unbelievable. In fact, in a period of just five weeks, a Chinese bamboo tree can grow to a height of 90 feet.

Now imagine if whoever planted the Chinese bamboo tree had given up on it and refused to water and fertilize it any longer. What if he had pulled out the seedling to just check if the seed is still there? What if he had got discouraged and given up all together saying nothing will ever come out of his efforts, his daily watering and his periodic fertilizing? If he had given up and thrown in the towel, nothing would have germinated. Not because he was not doing the right things initially, but because he gave up too soon on his efforts.

Success in life works mostly like that. In fact, it is another major principle that you have to learn in life. You must not give up on your daily watering and daily fertilizing. When you are daily investing and growing yourself, when you are daily adding worth to yourself, then you are right on your way to becoming a champion so soon. You need to keep that faith.

I remember as a young Pastor working to grow my Church, I was doing everything I knew how to do to grow my Church. I remembered giving myself a daily target of sharing a hundred fliers inviting different people to fellowship. That meant I had to see at least one hundred different people each day and invite them to fellowship. What was the result after one year? How many people came to Church? Not one person.

Eventually, after keeping to this routine for a long time, certain things began to happen in our ministry that saw us grow to a population of about five thousand people within three years. Now what do you think would have happened if I had given up? What would have happened if after one year of inviting thousands of people to church and no one showed up, I had simply given it all up, I would have given up the five thousand who later came too. I hope you understand it. Your manifestation is buried in the daily seeds you are sowing right now. You have to keep nurturing it and keep believing that it will come up right and it will germinate correctly. Harvest is near.

"Champions aren't made in gyms. Champions are made from something they have deep inside them-a desire, a dream, a vision. They have to have the skill, and the will. But the will must be stronger than the skill." (Muhammad Ali)

HIGHLIGHTS
FROM CHAPTER SEVEN

1. Everyman on earth is equally wealthy because every man on earth has equal time each day.

2. Many so called learned and educated people are still busy going to places of worship and religious centres to beg God to give them something that he has already given them.

3. The key to realizing and to maximizing the vast amount of wealth that you have got is called conversion.

4. Without work there will be no blessing. Work brings out the potential in you.

5. Every problem in the world is only making a demand or request for someone with a commensurate amount of value.

6. Whatever amount of time that you convert to add value to yourself is never a wasted time. Time is never wasted if you are using it to add value to yourself.

7. The value you have created will later work for you. The value you have created in yourself will later run returns to you.

CHAPTER 8
···

HOW TO USE YOUR NET WORTH TO BECOME THE MOST SIGNIFICANT PERSON ON EARTH

My dear friend, I am so happy that you have come this far in this book already. There is no doubt that you have acquired so much information which is going to change your entire life completely. I know you are ready to begin building your net worth now.

In the last chapter, we discussed on how you can determine your net worth and attain it. We discussed how you can determine what value you want to be on the earth and achieve those goals. We also looked at principles with which you can build strategies to unearth the potentials within.

What you have discovered so far in this book is not enough, I have got more. In this chapter, I want to teach you how you can use your net worth to achieve significance. I will show you how with your net worth you can become one of the most significant people on the earth.

Why am I teaching this? Okay, let me give you a simple task. Can you take a pen and paper right now and write out the names of the fifteen richest people in the world. Were you able to do that? Probably not. Why were you not able to? Because not everyone is truly significant. There may be a lot of people with money, but money necessarily does not give significance. What makes you truly significant is that you are actively and proactively solving a problem. I hope you get it. Your net worth affords you this rare opportunity. Net worth is not about building an empire, building your net worth is about being an answer to the cry and problems of humanity, that is what makes you significant.

YOUR NET WORTH IS FROM ADDED VALUE

Your net worth comes mainly from added value either to yourself, to others or to the product or service that you are producing.

Let us say for example that you are a caterer and that you bake cakes. As a caterer, you are spending a lot of time studying how cakes are done. Let's say you devote two hours of your time everyday into studying cake and finding designs and techniques that will give you a competitive brand. You are simply devoting enormous amount of time to the art of baking cakes, how to make better cakes, how to make cakes that are healthy and suitable to buy etc. You are also discovering in the process how to find and use new ingredients for cake, how to create fashionable cakes, how to promote, sell and market it.

If you study two hours every day about the subject, nobody necessarily sees that effort except people who are very close to you. However you should know that what you are doing, though not seen by anyone is adding value to you and your products, you are creating value for yourself.

Even though right now there is no money to pay for a car you want to buy, though there is no money to pay for your house or you are living in a rented house, though there is no money to pay for comfort and luxury, you have something which is greater, you have value.

You don't need to worry about that. You know that when a farmer goes to the farm, he takes a seed and plants it. In all cases, it takes some time for the planted seed to germinate, to grow and to begin to bear fruit.

It is same thing with each and every one of us, we need to keep on converting time. Even though the fruit is not visible easily and immediately, the most important thing is to keep on creating value. You are converting your time into value. When the right time comes like the tree that is planted, its time will come anyway.

When you don't stop working on that field, when you don't stop adding water to it, when you don't stop tending your ground. If you keep on adding value to yourself, if you keep on converting the wealth of time into added value to yourself, one day, definitely one day, your time will come.

ANNOUNCE YOURSELF TO THE WORLD

Another aspect that is critical as you keep on adding value to yourself is to pay attention to something very critical. That which is also critical is to announce to the world what your value is and what your products are. Do not be silent about what you do, let the whole world get to meet you through your products.

For example, I wrote this book which is in your hand right now, if I have not found a way to bring it out and let the world know the value of what it possesses, it probably would have remained as mere manuscripts under my pillow. So as you are adding value to yourself and if you are doing anything really worthwhile, you must learn how to advertise yourself, how to promote yourself, how to look for partners, how to talk to other people who might be interested. You must find a way to convince the world or to showcase to the world the ability that your product possesses or that it has.

You must through strategy and ideas find ways by which your product will stop being a local brand but a global brand. So as an example again, if there is anyone who is more renowned than you in the cake industry right now, they probably have added more value to themselves than you in the world of baking or they have found ways to convince the world that their cake is superior to yours. That is why everyone still patronises them and not you.

Get out of your small thinking, get on the big stage, the world wants to hear and see you. The world wants to know what you can do. The world wants to see your potentials. The world wants to see your value and whatever you carry within yourself. A lot of people want to win, but many more people are winning in the dark. No one knows them, of their achievements or who they are. Do not be quiet about your successes and achievements so far.

Can you imagine that among the twenty richest men

in the world today, there are so many you do not even know their names. Yet, there are a lot more who though may not be as rich as the first twenty, but have more significance and are influencing more people. That is true net worth.

If you are developing yourself all round, that added value becomes your worth. It becomes your net worth, even though it has not given you money yet, it's already an added value. The only thing needed for that value to become money is for somebody to take note of you or your product one day. When you have worked extremely hard to create your value, then all you need is for somebody to see you, perceive you or notice you or for you to just speak.

The mere fact that you have added value to yourself, the fact that you are a skilled expert right now, the fact that you already know what to do and you know it better than any other person, the fact that you are more prepared than any other person has placed your value and your net worth above that of every other person too.

Your manifestation to the world is just a matter of time, your physical wealth is just a matter of time. So your real wealth and real worth is that added value that has been put within you.

How to become significant
AND TRULY WEALTHY

Wealth and riches is not just having access to tangible money or when you have the physical money in your hand. Money and other forms of physical wealth are things which come later on. Your real worth is the added value. That is your worth. That is what makes you significant. It is not how many zeros are after a large figure in your bank account or being number one on the list of world's richest. Those things are good, but there is something more.

Let's talk about Bill Gates for example. Bill is the richest man in the world but he became the richest man in the world not because he was busy searching for money. What made Bill Gates the richest man in the world is Microsoft. Microsoft is his added value, the time that he converted in making himself skillful by creating value in himself and also by creating his product.

So in essence, it is the skill, the know-how, the knowledge of Microsoft that is his net worth. He is actually worth more than the amount people are saying he is worth now. Earlier in the book, I quoted Bill Gates' net worth in 2016. In that year, Bill Gates total money was put at 76.7 billion dollars. Well, if you understand the principle we have just discussed, you will understand that he is worth much more than that.

The 76.7 billion dollars that the entire world is talking about is what they can see. It is the tangible, physical, material money. That is just the amount that has been produced but the worth itself is in him.

He has been able to create a worth within himself which is worth much more than that value. What do I mean? You cannot produce a value physically that you have not attained unto within yourself.

Let me explain with this illustration. If a man's value within can be quantified, if the worth of a man can be placed in numbers or percentage, then we will say that a man whose value within him is worth a million dollars cannot produce more than a million dollars physically.

The worth of what he will generate physically cannot be more than a million dollars when quantified and in total. If you give such a man a billion dollar worth of asset to manage, because he is a million dollar man on the inside, he will reduce whatever thing you give to him that is more than a million dollars into that amount.

A man will do everything to reduce or upgrade the value of everything around him into the worth of his person or the worth of the value he carries. In same manner, if a man is a billion dollar man, if the worth of the value he has placed and created within himself can be quantified, and the worth of that value is estimated at a billion dollars. If you put such a man into an environment that is empty and where there is nothing, if you put such a man into the midst of the desert, all you need to do is give that man some time, a few years perhaps, he will raise the value of everything around him into the worth of what he carries within him. Within a few years, everything within that desert will be worth billions of dollars. I hope you understand that truth because it is potent enough to change your life. So can I ask you based on this understanding? How much are you really worth? I am not talking about the money in your bank account, I am talking about the worth of value you possess within.

YOUR NET WORTH IS THE VALUE YOU CARRY WITHIN

Your total net worth is the total value within you right now. Concerning Bill Gates, the fact that he was able to create and generate that value in himself, the skill, the expertise that he has developed in himself, that is his net worth. His net worth is the value created in him. It is how much time he used judiciously, how much conversion he was able to do with his time. That is his net worth. Money is only a manifestation later on. Cash and bank accounts are just physical manifestation.

So we shouldn't run after money. It is not money that makes us rich, it is not money that determines our worth. Money only comes to confirm the worth we already created in ourselves. Your net worth could be accessed differently.

Somebody accessed the net worth of Bill Gates and said he's 60 billion dollar rich but that is not his worth. He is worth much more than that, his worth is much greater than the money. His net worth is the revolution that he created. It is the fame, it is the aura, the name he created for himself. It is the fact that he made computer available to everybody. That is his worth, that is his real net worth. His net worth is more than that money.

I see a lot of people do not understand this and that is why they go about seeking money the wrong way. If you study the life of billionaires and significant people all over the world who acquired true wealth you will see a different pattern in them. They were people who were not striving to be rich, they were only striving to add value to themselves and solve a problem. They only wanted to be a solution to the crisis that they have observed and what they can do to provide solutions. An example of such a man is Henry Ford.

Henry Ford in his life time determined that he was going to make automobile accessible and affordable to every family in the United States. That was a very high dream at the time, it is like saying right now that you want to make private jet at the cost that we have it today affordable to every family and every single person on the earth. Many people will call you crazy. Even though that is what is going to happen eventually, it is unfathomable for many minds today.

However, crazy as it seemed, Henry Ford believed that he could achieve it, he believed that he could do it and he went about adding value to himself in that area. He began looking for ways to design and recreate inexpensive automobile engines, he began to redesign the body parts so that cars could be affordable to government workers, artisans and farmers. His dream was that in his lifetime, cars and automobiles will stop being the exclusive right and affluence of the rich.

He worked extremely hard for long years and eventually his dream and determination began to pay off. He created the Ford Company which began to sell cars to people at affordable prices. Henry Ford was solving a popular problem that in no time he became very popular and the favorite of everyone. A lot of people were buying his cars and he was also adding more value to himself and to his company. In no time, Henry Ford became a billionaire and one of the most powerful men on the planet at his own time.

What am I saying? True wealth does not come to you because you chose to aggressively pursue more money, true wealth comes to you because you chose to keep adding value to yourself and your product. The value in return will create any form of wealth for you.

This is why wealthy people often boast of their ability to recreate all of their wealth again if everything they currently have gets stolen from them. Have you heard any incredibly rich man talk in this lines before? Rich men often claim that their worth is not in what they carry in their pocket, their true worth cannot be carried in a wallet neither can it be written on any bank cheque, their true wealth and worth is in the wealth that they have taken the time to create within themselves.

Same reason why a man like Bill Gates could give out all the money he has and he would still be respected, in fact he would still be rich. He could afford to give out 40 billion dollars of his wealth because it is not the money that created his worth. What created his worth is the value he has already created through the conversion of time.

Another man who operates with the guidelines and this principle is Warren Buffet. Warren buffet was also estimated to be worth 74.2 billion dollars in 2016. Some years earlier, he gave out 30 billion dollars, a large percentage of his entire monetary worth to charity because it is not the money that creates his worth. Because of that singular act of donation, he dropped drastically from the list of the World's richest. The amazing thing was that within a few years, in fact within a space of less than three years, he was back to being among the top six richest people in the world again.

The worth of all of these men that I have cited is in the value they have been able to generate in themselves. The time they have been able to convert to become who they are.

The topic of our discussion and the subject we have focused on in this chapter is how you create and generate your net worth.

CREATE YOUR NET WORTH THROUGH YOUR TIME CURRENCY

Money does not create your worth. You create your net worth through your time currency. Every man has time, nature has made that available to every man on the earth. You already have currency and that currency is time. That currency is more important than money currency. Money itself is a currency but the currency of time is much more important than the money currency.

As a matter of fact money is created out of the time currency, money is a product of time. Money is created from time. So if you have the most important currency; the time currency, you don't have to look for another currency any more. What you must however do is to convert the time currency into cash currency.

The thing you need to do is to remember the word conversion, that is the most important word in the world. The ability to convert every minute, every second of your life into a tangible product, the ability to convert your time into a good or into a service is what is creating your net worth. The ability to convert every minute, every second of your life either into tangible product or tangible service is what creates net worth for you.

Even if you are not converting your time into a product or service immediately, you must convert every minute of your day into added value to yourself and for yourself. That added value is your worth, adding value to yourself is creating your net worth.

If you are using that time like I did in writing this book to create value for others, that converted time used in creating value for others is creating your net worth.

For example, you are reading this book right now, you

could have read a couple of other books I have written and this could be the first time you are reading a book from me. The truth is I spent hours creating each of those books you came across. So much of my resources, energy and time went into creating each of the books you ever came across.

I converted the time into the product called books. Many hours of my time each day is spent converting into one form of product or the other. I spend many sleepless nights creating value for other people. Now, how does that turn to my net worth? You may ask.

The time I spent in writing books and materials is my net worth. You don't pay for that, you are not paying for that. I'm sure you know you did not pay for my hours of preparations. Why did I choose to dedicate my life to creating enormous value for people every day? I have platforms in which I spend many hours of my life every day teaching, nurturing and instructing people. These people too are not paying anything.

Why are you giving people many hours of your life for free? Because net worth is more important than money. Please my dear friend, always remember that net worth is more important than money. Money comes after net worth has been created. Money only shows its face after enough value has been generated. Money is an aftermath of true wealth.

Let me instruct you on another urgent matter. Let me teach you something else. Are you still asking me why I am giving so much of myself, so much of my time and so much of my resources for free? I understand something that you need to understand too.

Created value or added value is more important than

the money you could pay me. I am getting more, I am receiving more by adding value to you. I receive far more in worth and value by adding value to people than could ever come to me as money. There is no money equivalent to the value I receive when I send value out to people from me.

I am receiving more by adding value to you. I am receiving more net worth than any money you could pay me. Let me tell you the principle behind this. When I get your attention through my books or teachings, when you read from me or listen to me with the hours of your day, something happens to you. Something remarkable begins to occur, you begin to experience definite changes in your life.

Your eyes are open, your minds are open, you are becoming the person you dreamt of becoming. Your life is changing. That is just what you are getting. Imagine the ripple effects of the changes that you experience through my materials on other people around you. Imagine the ripple effects on your family, on your work and on your nation. Now what do I get? What do I benefit in return?

What I get is net worth. Returns come to me as net worth. How does that turn to my net worth, I'm sure you are asking again? Let me explain to you. I get net worth from you being better from the changes you experience in your life.

Please do not forget this fact that I am about to tell you. Whenever you create changes in the life of somebody, whenever you add value to someone, that person whom you have added value to remembers the source of that value that has been added to him. Can you go back now and read the last sentence again carefully?

YOU BECOME SIGNIFICANT WHEN
YOU ADD VALUE TO PEOPLE

When you add value to somebody, that person knows who has added that value to him. Even if he wants to deny it, he will not forget where the source of those changes in his life came from. So my net worth is coming from you to me in terms of respect and in terms of honour.

Net worth is not only measured by money, you are not giving me money but I am earning your honour. In the second place, I am earning your respect. Thirdly I am earning your trust and gaining your followership.

There are so many people around the world who right now want to listen to me on daily basis or who cannot but read one of my books within a week. Some people always love to get resources and materials from me for their personal growth and development. Now, if you cannot do without my words and the value I'm adding to you anymore, then I have increased in my net worth. So you are following me and I have increased in the net worth of my followership.

This is why successful businesses do not pursue monetary gain, rather they pursue followership. Successful businesses have learnt this secret and will do anything to gain your trust and attention. If at any time, they provide you the wrong service, they will go to any extent to appease you and to ensure they do not lose you as a customer.

It is not necessarily your money those companies and businesses are after, they are much more interested in your loyalty to them. They understand that when you love them to a great extent, you will also bring your friends and family to buy from them. Because your family members love you and you love them, those ones too will bring their friends and recommend them to other people. In no time, they are everywhere and their name means something to everyone in the market.

Now imagine a company which has grown in worth and followership from a few hundred people to several millions of people bringing out a new product, several millions of people will buy from them, hence they have converted part of that worth into cash. Oh, how I wish that more people will become wise and learn this secret. Stop wasting your life, stop pursuing money. Money will finish, but the net worth you add, once added to you will always flourish and increase.

Do not focus on money, men of little worth are the ones who always focus on money. They want to extort people and get money from everyone at all cost. When you see a man like that, understand that he is a shallow thinker. Such men can even sacrifice their name on the altar of cash, just to have anything within their wallet. When a man like that meets you for the first time, he is already thinking how much dollars he can get from you or rob you off. Such thinking is what has also produced armed robbers, and thieves, scammers and pickpockets.

It is such thinking that makes a politician use his highly exalted office to loot his people, forgetting that he has a name and reputation to leave behind for his sons unborn. It is such poor thinking that makes the manager of a company cheat his co-workers and the people he has been entrusted to lead.

Instead of putting your focus on money, you should put your focus on adding value, on solving a problem that needs to be solved for the world. What problems can you solve right now? The good news is, problems are abundant in the world. Problems are being created every day, so in essence wealth too is being created every day. When you solve a problem, money will follow you as a by-product.

Earlier, I was talking to you about the net worth I acquire by investing myself in people and adding value to people. Do you remember the things that I already highlighted as my profit? Great! One of them is gaining the trust and followership of more and more people. Now, remember it's not just one person but thousands of people we are talking about, I am richer by thousands of more people every day that are either watching my numerous programs or reading my books or visiting me as an individual.

Before I started speaking or writing books, many people did not know me. Since I started releasing products and finding new ways to add value to people, many people have discovered me, ignorance about me is disappearing. Light, illumination and understanding is coming to people. Thanks to my investment and my added value.

Again, still proceeding on what my net worth is with adding value to people, a lot of people who follow me are in different parts and different countries of the world. Can you imagine just because I invest some hours of my day to reaching many people, I am harvesting `disciples, I am harvesting followers, many people who believe in me are simultaneously in more than one hundred countries of the world at the same time. I'm reaching out to more than a hundred countries at the same time. My influence is growing in over one hundred countries at the same time. Think about that.

It is not impossible for you to do the same. You can achieve more feats than that. When you add enough value to yourself and you in turn add value to other people, your presence can become felt in many nations of the world. You can influence the world with your products, you can become a person that cannot be ignored.

Imagine that as I write about this right now, Bill gates is in many homes around the world at same time. His presence is felt in Italy and he is also present in homes in Spain at same time. He is in France and at same time in Abuja, Nigeria. Why? He has found a way to successfully add value to a lot of people simultaneously and at same time.

Through his product, he is able to influence virtually every nation on earth without leaving the comfort of his home. You may dislike him, you may hate him because he is an American, you may not like the fact that he is an atheist or that he does not speak your language, one thing is certain however, you cannot ignore Bill Gates. You have to use his product or someone has to use his product to help you, period. That is the net worth of a single man. That is what he has been able to gain as a result of adding value to other people. That is how immense his net worth is. That is how great a man he has become. That is also the extent of his reach, his ability to be in almost every nation on earth at the same time.

MY CHALLENGE TO YOU

I challenge you to seek ways by which you can become a man like that. I challenge you to come out with a product that can be used by every nation on earth. I challenge you to write a book which will be found on desks in every home. I challenge you to sing a song which will be heard in most moving cars in the country. I challenge you to come out with a recipe which will make many look forward to dinner. Is it possible for you to create a company, perhaps a restaurant which is everyone's delight and the talk of town? Can you improve on what you do right now so that it becomes the demand on more than three continents of the world?

Remember, there is nothing anybody has done that you too cannot do, you only need to add same values that they added to themselves.

Furthermore, when you begin to produce results, when you begin to bring out your project, when you begin to produce your fruits, when you begin to add value to others, when your gifts begin to add value to others, when you begin to produce your product and services, we together are changing the world. We are changing the face of the world, we are together setting a new pattern and leaving a legacy for our children and our children's children.

The problem of hunger that we refuse to solve now will be the problem of hunger that our children will face and battle with. The crisis of the environment now that we leave unresolved will be what our children will have to tackle or they will also leave that behind for generations after them. When we cannot create electricity and solve the lingering problem of darkness once and for all in our communities in Africa, then the new babies that will be born after we are gone will open their eyes into a world full of darkness.

What am I saying? Every one of us has a solution within him right now. I carry worth within me and you do too, when you convert these worth into products, into goods and services, when these services solve the problem in the world then we make the world a better place. Changing the world is as easy as that. Changing the world is simply every man making his contribution through his net worth.

In addition, God knows about everything I am investing in people and in you, even if you will not say thank you. For example a lot of people express to me how much they love me so much even though they didn't love me before they started reading my books or listening to me through other media.

So net worth is more important than money.

Apart from the fact that people will reward me, you remember what scriptures said. The scriptures encouraged every one of us to gather up our treasure in heaven where there will be no thieves, where there will be no robbery, no ants to eat it or destroy it.

YOUR MONEY IS TEMPORARY,
YOUR NET WORTH IS ETERNAL

I remember losing my wallet once. Every vital document that was in the wallet with a lot of money was stolen. With just one encounter with a thief all of my money was gone. That is what happens when we only lay up our treasures as currency and as gold, you may one day wake up to discover that all your worth is now useless.

Many years ago, some friends encouraged me to put some money in Nigerian banks since I am Nigerian, though I reside in Ukraine. They said words of flattery that eventually convinced me to put some sum of money into the bank in Nigeria. Truth is, within a few years and especially when the naira sharply declined, all the money lost value. I do not know what that money will be worth again now. In fact, I suspect the money has become so useless that the bank has not contacted me in a long time, I have not bothered to ask what happened to my money either. I doubt that if by today's economy and exchange rate, the recent worth of that money can buy a single tire for my car. That is what this world means and that is the worth of this world.

If you must use the worth of this world to create a net worth for yourself, then you must start thinking immediately of conversion and adding value to other people. Adding value to others is more important than the money they will get from you if you were to give them money. Of course, the best we all got from our parents was not their money, it was the value they instilled within us.

Now, let us shift our discussion to money, let us talk about money for a moment. I know you are probably wondering how you will generate money for yourself in all of this. You are probably wondering about the bills you have to pay, your rent and mortgage, your loans and how to purchase fuel for your car. Am I correct? I understand you perfectly.

We still need money to live, I still need money to operate, I still need money to function. How do I get the money? Listen closely how I get the money. If I were interested in having some money, I could easily take any of the books I have written and sell them. The main aim of writing my books however had never been money, my motivation for doing what I do will never be money. As a matter of fact, I have never made money from the books I write, other people do. What am I saying? I am trying to show you the possibility of converting the worth of these books into some cash or money. Again, money is not my interest, cash is not my interest, I'm not interested in that. I have come to understand the principles of building wealth and increasing value than that.

So what I did was to tell people and anyone who is interested in the sale of my books to come have discussions with me. I want such people to come to me and have discussions on channels by which the books can be distributed and they can make money for themselves from the book sales. I am happy that a lot of people are doing that and it is generating a source of income for many people right now. I have told people time and again to pick any of my topics that they are interested in, package them into CDs, package them into teaching materials and live off them.

Turn yourself into a motivational speaker or turn yourself into a life coach. Go and conduct seminars, teachings and let people pay for it. Use me to make your own money, be a distributor, sales man etc. If I had wanted to, I could use the materials I have prepared to make my own money.

I write my books, I produce teachings, those are ways by which I could have made money. I could produce money from many of these materials. Like I said earlier, I write my books but I don't even make money from the books. I'm not interested in making money from the books. Anybody who sells my books make money from the books. If my interest is to convert resources to money, that would not be difficult.

For example I could organise a conference or world-wide seminar. I could invite people to come and they pay for it. But you know money is secondary, it will come sooner or later. I understand this principle and I employ it. If you create in yourself value and you create value in others, money will come. Especially if you know how to create time into product and services, money will surely come.

Money came to Bill Gates not because he looked for money. He only created net worth. Money will always run after net worth. Money will always run after created value, so it is not when you run after money that you make money. It is when you create value, when you add value, when you create net worth that money will run after you. When you run after money then you lack the time to create value, you don't have time to create a value chain.

If you are running after money, you don't have time to add value to yourself or to add value to others. It's a cheap way of living, it's a cheap substitution. That is a cheap but costly exchange. I hope you understand that.

The real thing you are supposed to be doing like I'm doing right now is to be busy creating value. How are you going to embark on this? How are you going to add value to yourself? How are you going to create a net worth within you? I dare you right now to arise and start doing something, start creating value within yourself, within others and converting your values into a product. When you do this, no doubt the future becomes guaranteed.

HIGHLIGHTS
FROM CHAPTER EIGHT

1. There may be a lot of people with money, but money necessarily does not give significance. What makes you truly significant is that you are actively and proactively solving a problem.

2. Your net worth mainly is coming from added value. Either to yourself, to others or to the product or service that you are producing.

3. Announce to the world what your value is and what your products are. Do not be silent about what you do, let the whole world get to meet you through your products.

4. Get out of your small thinking, get on the big stage, the world wants to hear and see you.

5. A man will do everything to reduce or upgrade the value of everything around him into the worth of his person or the worth of the value he carries.

6. Do not focus on money, men of little worth are the ones who always focus on money.

7. Money will always run after net worth. Money will always run after created value.

CHAPTER 9

....

KEY AREAS TO BUILD YOUR NET WORTH

Congratulations! No doubt you are armed with so much knowledge now about building your net worth. I can say with confidence that if you will put all that you have learnt into practice, you will be one of the most significant people in this generation. You will not only be a person of worth, you will be a person of great net worth.

Do you still remember the difference between worth and net worth? Great! You must always remember that. I am also sure you read the last chapter carefully where we talked about how you can be the most significant person on earth using the power of your net worth.

In this last chapter, I will be discussing with you some key important areas for you to build your net worth.

WHAT IS THE GREATEST HINDRANCE TO BUILDING YOUR NET WORTH?

If you must build your net worth in the key areas that I will discuss with you shortly, then you must avoid the common pit people fall into. This common pit is the pit of being obsessed with immediate gain.

A lot of people want instant gratification and immediate pleasure that they sacrifice anything, including their big vision, their long term goal. This is the singular greatest hindrance to building net worth.

The real thing you are supposed to be doing like I'm doing right now is to be busy creating value. And in order to do that, you must be willing to make sacrifices, you must be willing to sacrifice immediate gains for long term goals. You must be willing to choose value over money, personal growth over salary. People who are looking for money do very funny and meaningless things, what do they do? Now think about this, such people exchange and mortgage their time which is their life for salary.

A lot of people in the world today find it convenient to go out and give out their time in exchange for money and salary. Such people are blindfolded by salary and instant money. What a shame, what a pity.

Many more people think that instant money is more important to them right now. But really, what they have done is that they have sold out their lives for property. What many people have done is that they have mortgaged part of their entire existence for a little salary.

Please understand me, my dear friend, are you reading very closely? Do you understand what I'm talking about? I do not want you to have regrets at the end of your life. At the end of your life, I do not want you to look back at your life and what you found were meaningless ruins and traces of a life that had no meaning.

The way Bill Gates did it or that I am doing it or that a lot of other people in the world are doing it is not by using our time to slave out for other people. We are not giving out our lives, which is our time in meaningless pursuit or the pursuit of salary. We are nobody else's slaves.

Do not become a slave to somebody; do not become a slave to your employer or to your boss. You do not need to sell out your time but you can convert your time into added value for yourself. When you refuse to use your time to work for somebody else but you use that time to convert and add value into yourself, you are not losing your life, you are not losing your time. You are actually reproducing your time. And when you keep on doing it, it goes from reproduction into multiplication. So the added value to yourself is not lost, it's not going away. It's reproducing something in you.

Earlier I said this, the hours I use every day in creating value is not what am being paid for or getting money for, rather what is creating my net worth is through multiplication, the duplication and the replication of lives that daily occur through me. I am multiplying, not money but people.

Now imagine I just go to work for salary, what happens then is that I simply get a little bit of compensation for a life that is given away.

A lot of people get deceived thinking salary is more important than net worth. The only thing we can compare such a life to is getting momentary pleasure from cocaine in exchange for a lifetime of addiction. Yes, the same life that people on drug addiction live is the same life that people who live on salary also live. It is all about sacrificing the big picture, the big vision, the bigger goal for what seems suitable at the moment.

Do not sell out your future for salary

I am telling you not to sacrifice the big goal in your life for momentary pleasure, I am telling you that creating your net worth by adding value to yourself and adding value to others is more important than money. I am pleading with you not to sell out your future for the salary you are currently being paid.

How many times have you wanted to go develop yourself, or you wanted to go add value to yourself that the only thing stopping you is your salaried job? Every time you choose finite money over infinite value, you have not chosen wisely.

A lot of people try to justify the reason why they slave out their lives in paid jobs with the excuse of having to provide for their families etcetera. But consider this, you probably spend about eight hours every day in somebody else' assignment. The question is, how many hours do you spend each day in your own assignment and in your life calling? What do you do when you get home from work? What do you do in the late hours of evening? What do you do when your kids are in bed, just in case your excuse is that of having to care for kids? What do you do when you wake up in the early hours of the morning?

My dear friends, those moments are the most critical moments of your life. If you will not slave for somebody else the rest and full days of your life,if you will not live on salary and die in pension, if you will create worth in this life that will be remembered after you are gone, if your life will hold any net worth and any value while you are yet alive, then you must pay attention to these critical moments of your life I have mentioned to you. When you go to work for somebody else or for the government in the early mornings and late afternoons, then you must immediately sit down to work on your own life assignment in the evenings, late into the night and early in the morning.

It is unfortunate that a lot of people come back from their jobs and salaried works, and immediately sit to watch the Television. It is also unfortunate because many of these people who should rather take advantage of the opportunities that the week end brings are wasting that time too. Many will not busy themselves creating values and products, they would rather be away on unnecessary parties and in sport stadiums. What a life! What a waste!

Adding value to your own product, to your own service is more important than money. Money will come later on. But develop a skill. Develop a skill like Bill Gates developed a skill. Develop a skill like Steve Jobs developed a skill. Develop a skill like Mark Zuckerberg developed a skill too.

BUILD YOUR NET WORTH IN THE AREA OF SOLITUDE

Convert your time, yes, do not sell out your time. Convert that time into investing into yourself. Convert that time into adding value into yourself, convert that your time into adding value later to other people. Convert that time into adding value to your own product and service. That is how you create net worth, you are already expensive, you are already big, big things will follow later. Do not sell out yourself cheap.

Let me give you an example of myself. When I became

a Christian, like every other Christian I prayed every day and I read the Bible every day.

I discovered that each time I prayed for about two hours or three hours without a break, I began to feel the anointing of God, I felt the goose bumps and the anointing. For me to feel the presence of God, I needed to pray at least two or three hours every day. Sometimes I needed to pay the sacrifice of upwards of four hours in prayer.

Because of that, each time I wanted to go and preach at church, in a conference or at any location, I would usually pray for a period of about four to six hours. Normally I would pray about six hours a day before I go to preach, it was the sacrifice I needed for me to begin to feel the anointing. I was doing that until I discovered something. Do you want to know what I discovered? Okay, here it is.

I discovered a secret and a principle that is called solitude, a process of putting myself away and practicing a discipline of being alone all by myself in a particular place for a very long time. I started practicing solitude.

Once a month I would go away, lock everything away from me, or rather myself away from everything. During the week of solitude, I had no access to my wife, children, staff or any living person. There was nothing and no one to distract me. In my week of solitude, I ensured I was praying for a minimum of fourteen hours every day of that week.

I was not just blabbing words in prayer, I was also studying and reading. I was practicing the discipline of just being in the presence of God for a minimum of fourteen hours each day. Some days during the week, I ensured I was working for a period of eighteen hours. Sometimes I would just be praying.

I did that for a full year, then I tried it again the second year. By the end of that time, I was getting some results in the ministry and in my personal life.

But when I did that continuously for eight years, ten hours to fourteen hours of praying, studying and waiting on God each week of my solitude, the results became unquantifiable. That was not all, apart from the week of solitude, every month I would seek out another fourteen hours within the month for personal study. My solitude was taking a whole week out, at times three days, sometimes five days and very often seven days.

Those days of solitude were minimum of three days, I placed myself under the strict discipline of taking out time just to be in the presence of God every day. So out of the four weeks in a month, I would always take one week alone to lock myself up and to just practice solitude.

You know what I discovered? After doing that for 8 years, you know what began to happen to me? Remember what I said in the beginning, in order for me to go and preach I needed to feel the presence of God. To feel that presence of God, I needed a personal sacrifice of praying for about four to 6 hours. However, when I had spent more than 10,000 hours or more in solitude just in the presence of God, after more than eight years of consistently practicing solitude, something different began to happen to me, I began to have experiences like I was soaked and drenched in water-like substance without praying. It was like I was soaked and immersed.

Right now, the result of that discipline is that I don't need to pray one minute to sense God, to feel that same presence I was praying for six hours to feel. Right now it's like God soaked me and drenched me in his presence. Do you know the way you soak a cloth in water, same way it was like I was soaked in the grace and anointing of God.

I just need to tune in now, just like you tune in into radio wave and at the right frequency, you begin to pick out clear sounds and what you want to hear. Right now I just need to switch my wave from the natural into God.

For example if I just want to know what is happening to somebody somewhere, or if I want to be able to discern what is going to happen somewhere or in a particular situation, I can tune in and I will get a message.

I see Jesus every day at will, I am his friend. Right now I live in God, it's like He is my skin. I have converted so much hours, so much time into his presence that now I carry that presence automatically.

The same thing with preaching also, I have over 1 million messages that I have preached and that have been recorded, that's like over 10, 000 hours of preaching also. So when you hear me preach, it's not like you are listening to any other regular pastor preaching. Why is this? Because I have converted so much time into solitude, I have built my net worth in solitude.

That is the point, that is what I'm saying, conversion is the key. My net worth has increased greatly with God. My increased net worth in spiritual things is what makes me to be so close to the Holy Spirit. It is that sacrifice of building and increasing my net worth in the spiritual realm that makes it easy to be able to hear from God easily.

That is about creating net worth. For that net worth

to become money is a secondary thing. For eight years I didn't feel that presence of God easily. Even though I was already a Pastor, I could not hear God or be able to switch to the spirit quite easily, I could not see Jesus every day at will. I couldn't do it, it couldn't happen to me. But now because I've converted so much time in the presence of God, I now carry that presence of God. That manifested presence of God now in me is my net worth. As it is in the spiritual things, so it is in the physical things.

You can create net worth for yourself in different areas. You can create net worth for yourself in your academics, you can create net worth for yourself in business, all you need to do is apply the same principle of adding value like I described above. You can also create net worth for yourself in the family.

BUILD YOUR NET WORTH IN THE AREA OF MARRIAGE AND FAMILY

Not many people know that they have to be able to create net worth for themselves in their family and marriage. Your marriage right now is a product of the net worth you and your spouse have chosen to build or not to build.

How do you build your net worth in marriage? It is by the amount of value you choose to add to your spouse. As a married person, you must understand that the amount of value you create in your spouse is what you eventually get to enjoy. If you do not seek to increase the amount of value that your spouse currently possesses, then you cannot enjoy the value that they can also produce.

I am glad that my wife is my foremost disciple. I am proud to see the fruit of the values I have added to her today. Adding value to her daily is my responsibility, it is my personal assignment to build worth in her and around her. Hence, I give her the best place in my daily routines and priorities, I adore her. You know the reason why? Because I am a wise man. I know that a happy wife will create a happy and angelic home. She will raise the best of children, she will make her husband happy. But a frustrated wife will make the environment in the home a place like hell. Such a wife will ensure her husband gets the full description of Lucifer on earth, so that he will recognise him easily when they eventually meet.

As a man, what net worth are you creating in your marriage? How are you adding value to your wife? How are you building her up? What are you doing to help her build her self-worth, self-esteem and self-confidence? Some foolish men would rather tear down from the little confidence their poor wives had already built before the unfortunate incidence of meeting them.

Many people applaud me when they see how I hold and applaud my wife. Many cannot believe it when I hold the doors of cars for her to enter or exit. I am always holding the hands of my wife whenever she has to ascend or descend the stairs. At an occasion, some people wrote to me asking for reasons why I could kneel in front of my wife in one of our pictures that went viral. What happened in the picture was that I was kneeling in front of my wife appreciating the woman she is to the world. Some ignorant men, especially some African men wrote to me asking why I could be doing that in front of my wife. Well, let me just put it this way. I know something that such men have not known. I know how to create worth and value in a woman that they have not discovered probably. Most importantly, I know that my life and my home will be the better for it if only I can add value and build net worth in my wife.

A common quote that has been used by several people with the author unknown goes thus

"Whatever you give a woman, she will make greater. If you give her sperm, she'll give you a baby. If you give her a house, she'll give you a home. If you give her groceries, she'll give you a meal. If you give her a smile, she'll give you her heart. If you give her trouble, she will give you hell. She multiplies and enlarges what is given to her."

A woman must also build net worth in her husband. She must encourage him, she must support him, she must offer her counsel with wisdom where necessary and be a pillar in her home. She must create the perfect atmosphere in the home and be a model for her children.

BUILD YOUR NET WORTH IN THE AREA OF SELF–DEVELOPMENT

Still talking about creating net worth, another area I create net worth for myself is in studying and self-development.

I study a minimum of three hours a day in all aspects that I want to learn and in self-development. Three hours of self-development is critical for me before my day can be termed successful. When I have more time to spare though and more free time, when I'm in solitude also, then my time of studying increases to about six hours and more.

When you do that every day for 10 years, you will become an expert. That is why you will never listen to me or read my books and be bored, you will not listen to Pastor Sunday and compare me with anybody.

If you listen to me at any time, you will understand that I am speaking from another realm.

Why? I have been doing that conversion of time. I have been studying, I have been labouring secretly. Through sweat and hard work, I have been putting treasures into myself.

Earlier in this book, I told you about a man called Malcolm Gladwell who did a research. The research showed that if you will invest 10,000 hours of yourself into practicing or studying anything you choose to study, you will become an expert. You will not just become an expert but you will become one of the best in the world. That is like doing something for about three to four hours a day for the next 10 years.

Can you imagine that a greater percentage of our world cannot create that personal discipline? Many people cannot focus on studying a particular line of interest for about three hours every day, and consistently for about ten years? This is the reason why mediocrity is so common and excellence is almost as rare as gold.

You can choose right now to create a particular time of study on any area and interest, and resolve to study on that for at least three hours every day for the next ten years. Malcolm Gladwell's research says if you do that, you will be among the top three percent in that field of endeavour within ten years. Can you imagine that?

Now, you must pay attention to this point. If you choose not to create that discipline to start studying and developing yourself now, the ten years will still pass anyway. However you will not be among the top three percent, you will be among the majority who are nobodies, the ninety seven percent who form the majority, the non-entity.

I did more than the required ten thousand hours. I was so harsh on myself in the area of my self-development. Wherever I have spoken and anywhere I speak, either at the United Nations building or Parliamentary buildings of nations or in churches and conferences, people simply wonder at me. Many people had their mouths opened agape, they couldn't believe the way and manner I spoke.

I went to the United States senate to speak, they couldn't believe that I was a pastor. I communicated in their language effectively. They were not used to Pastors talking like that.

This is the secret, I did not just invest over 10,000 hours reading the bible only. I was studying and pouring over books. I was digging up sources and comparing theories. I was studying biographies and learning how to make things work.

I did the same thing with the Bible. My interest as a preacher was not in repeating the sermons that everyone around the world was repeating. Many people are only repeating each other and telling stories. I wanted to be a different kind of preacher. I wanted to be a firebrand.

Many people who have heard me preach the Bible ask me what Bible I read. Many people have asked me how I got the things I teach or that perhaps I had a special Bible that I was reading which they are not aware of.

Again, this is the secret. I intentionally invested over 10000 hours of my life into studying and digging into the Bible. I was not reading the Bible with the lens of what somebody had taught me. I grew up in my Christian faith in the old soviet Union where Christianity was not allowed, so I had no access to teachings and preaching of other people, I had no access to people's doctrines etc. All I had was my Bible and a desperate desire to know God. That was all I had.

I converted that into over 10000 hours of study, I converted the passion into worth and value in reading the Bible only. I buried myself into working the word of God, and came out a genius.

BUILD THE NET WORTH OF YOUR MIND

So if you really want to control your world, don't just spend time studying the Bible alone. Study other things as well. In spite of any topic that I speak on, people often think I'm an expert only in that field, until they hear me speak on another subject and then begin to wonder. I have invested over 10000 hours to make myself the best as a preacher, to make myself the best as a human being also.

Daniel did not win over Babylon by just talking about the Bible. He did not become a prime minister in a foreign land by quoting scriptures. He was a politician, he had to understand the language of the people and the language of politics. He had to be wise in the wisdom of the land and the wisdom of God. That is how you can win.

If all you have got in your vocabulary is 'halleluyah' and 'Praise the Lord' you cannot really go far in life. You cannot reach certain set of people. There are some doors that will remain permanently closed to you.

You must be sound in the wisdom of God and in the wisdom required to walk in your calling. You must be wiser than the sons of Egypt and Babylon. You must be an expert that everyone wants to listen to. You must spread yourself and superimpose yourself on the world. The world must have no choice but to look up to you and to respect you.

Now you know the critical areas you must strive to build your net worth immediately. I have mentioned the net worth of the presence of God, the net worth of the Bible and the net worth of self-education.

Another net worth I created was that of creating a mega church. I have noticed over time that life is not in the struggles but in the secrets. The reason why you are struggling in any area of your life is because you have not taken the time to learn the secrets that is required. In building a mega church, I dedicated enough time to learning the secrets so much that the feat simply became something ordinary such as putting on a shirt. This I have shown by teaching many of my disciples how to also create mega churches and many of them have replicated same feats all over the world.

Building a mega church is like doing nothing, in fact it can be as enjoyable as drinking water. I understand though that a lot of people are struggling to do it simply because they have not taken the time to learn the secrets.

However, because I have invested more than twenty thousand hours in building a church, in mastering how to build a church, it became incredibly easy to do and to replicate. I took out that time in acquiring the skills on how to build a church. So that is another worth I have within me now. My worth doesn't have to be money, it is not about money.

When I decided I wanted to become a millionaire, I didn't need too much time for that. I only invested about two thousand hours to three thousand hours into studying about the laws of money and everything that pertains to money.

Now if you have read my book on money titled **"Money won't make you rich"** you will appreciate more the importance of putting value into yourself. A lot of people have said it is the best book they have ever read on finances. Even a late Zig Ziglar's team member wrote to appreciate the enormous treasure and wealth in the book. Many of the people who have read the book have said that the book is one of the best books that have ever been written on money in the whole world.

When I started talking about the kingdom, I spent so much time converting so much hours into studying the topic that another of my books titled 'Kingdom Driven Life' has been rated the best kingdom book that has ever been written in the whole world.

YOU CAN BE THE BEST IN ANY FIELD OF HUMAN ENDEAVOUR

Malcom Gladwell has proven it that if you will invest enough hours of time, at least 10000 hours into developing yourself in an area, you will become the best expert and your net worth will be so commendable. Every other thing will come to you and surround you.

So the question I have for you is this, 'in what area have you invested 10000 hours of your life'?

Whatever it is that you are doing that is not adding value to you has to be stopped immediately. You have to measure the things you do by how much value they are adding to you or to others. Every single minute must be converted to added value. You have to see the product that your life is bringing forth. Please, I plead with you again, be concerned about your net worth.

Jesus had so much net worth that even by the time he was at the young age of twelve, the Pharisees and Sadducees could not argue with him. He was full of wisdom, the same thing with Paul.

Unfortunately, many people just want to be religious. Many people can speak so well in tongues, in fact they can speak in tongues in different accents but they cannot speak to the real estate agent nor can they speak to the banker. Many know about the 'blood of Jesus' but know nothing about acquiring and signing a contract. So many people are just ignorant and this makes my heart to bleed again and again. Many people, most of the times just want to engage in religious activities, merely praying and going to church. What have empty religious activities benefited you except eye service. The only benefit is for people to recognise you that you are a good church member.

Don't waste your life on emptiness. Don't waste your life on empty activities and mundane life that has no profit. Don't be caught on a rocking horse, all motion, no progress. Don't become stuck in the religious mud of life.

The difference between people is only one thing, what they exchanged their time for. I really think you must note that carefully. Let me repeat it again for you in block letters. **The difference between people is only one thing, what they exchanged their time for.** The difference between people is in how they used their time.

While you were busy visiting from one prophetic house to the other, your colleague who understood the principles of life was adding value to himself and creating a product. I am also aware of the madness that young people also engage themselves in today in institutions of higher learning. Young people who otherwise should busy themselves in developing themselves and finding solutions to the problems of the common world, young people who should convert solitude into adding value into themselves are busy in religious jamboree and frenzy. Who will deliver these young ones?

WAYS YOU BENEFIT FROM YOUR NET WORTH

We have carefully established that your net worth will profit you in many ways and give you different gains, not just money.

Money is just one aspect of the reward, others could be authority, some other profits and rewards could be fame or respect or honour etc. When you add value you will have reward in more ways than money.

So the most important thing for you to know is that we are all equally endowed with time but what we become in life is what we do with that time.

God has given us his gift of time, our gift back to him is how we maximize that time. How we convert that time into real tangible product is what places you in life and determines your place.

The world will only pay attention to people who have created value, net worth for themselves and have through value solved problems for other people. The world will stand in awe of those who have turned their time into value chain.

The world will honour those who have through value

made life easier for humanity. Those are the only people that the world will listen to.

You can be a Christian for a long time and not be able to bring people to God like I can perhaps. When you cannot reason with certain people like I can or like someone else who has created value within himself, then the results will be different. I can get within a group of people and have discourses that they will respect, I can talk to them and speak directly to their needs. They will listen to me unlike someone who cannot.

Having been on the Bill Clinton Foundation, I sat on the same meeting with Bill Gates, with Warren Buffets, Richard Branson etc. In such meetings, you are not sitting with your Bible and your hymn book. You are not sitting there with your sermon jotters and your prayer shawl. The world is more than Bible. Even Paul was also quoting other writers of his time, Jesus was also quoting other great men that lived before him.

You have to keep on adding value to yourself. How will you find solution to medical problems, or electricity problems, or transport problems or issues of national development if you are reading only the bible?

For example if you want to find solutions to under-development in Africa, you must read economic books. Solutions to problems of poverty are found in financial books. You get more insight from the Bible when your mind is prepared.

The most important people are the ones who have invested enough time in themselves and created enough value in themselves through conversion of time.

I must emphasise one more time that the difference between people is what they exchange their time for.

So if you exchange your time for salary, you will only become a good worker.

If you only exchange your time for merry and pleasure, you have wasted your life. But if you exchange your time into creation of value, into adding value to yourself or value into others, if you will exchange your time into creation of product and services, into your calling, into your destiny and purpose, that is where your greatness is.

You should be able to critically analyse yourself. Don't let religion shut your mind down or make your head dull. Rather let religion increase you. Use faith in God to even produce more value. Let your faith in God be able to let you add better value to yourself and to others, let it make you create better product. Let your faith in God produce fruits.

Jesus said by their fruits we shall know them, not by their religiosity or going to church or by their tithe and offering. Set yourself free from the shackles of religion and become a believer for real. I had already written books on that, entire books have been written on conversion and how you can convert your ideas and inspirations into products. If you have not read them, you can look for these books. You will find material on how to become a good and fruitful believer.

Arise champion, arise to the call of God within you, arise to the need of your world, set loose that which God has placed within, build your net worth and use your net worth to transform the world. This generation is waiting for you.

I can't wait to see all that you will become and do through the information you have gathered from this book.

HIGHLIGHTS
FROM CHAPTER NINE

1. A lot of people want instant gratification and immediate pleasure that they sacrifice anything including their big vision and their long term goal. This is the singular greatest hindrance to building net worth.

2. A lot of people think that instant money is more important to them right now. But really, what they have done is that they have sold out their lives for property.

3. A lot of people get deceived thinking salary is more important than net worth.

4. How many hours do you spend each day in your own assignment and in your life calling? What do you do when you get home from work? What do you do in the late hours of the evening?

5. Build your net worth in the area of solitude.

6. Build your net worth in the area of self-development.

7. Build the net worth of your mind.

SUNDAY ADELAJA'S BIOGRAPHY

Pastor Sunday Adelaja is the Founder and Senior Pastor of The Embassy of the Blessed Kingdom of God for All Nations Church in Kyiv, Ukraine.

Sunday Adelaja is a Nigerian-born Leader, Thinker, Philosopher, Transformation Strategist, Pastor, Author and Innovator who lives in Kiev, Ukraine.

At 19, he won a scholarship to study in the former Soviet Union. He completed his master's program in Belorussia State University with distinction in journalism.

At 33, he had built the largest evangelical church in Europe — The Embassy of the Blessed Kingdom of God for All Nations.

Sunday Adelaja is one of the few individuals in our world who has been privileged to speak in the United Nations, Israeli Parliament, Japanese Parliament and the United States Senate.

The movement he pioneered has been instrumental in reshaping lives of people in the Ukraine, Russia and about 50 other nations where he has his branches.

His congregation, which consists of ninety-nine percent white Europeans, is a cross-cultural model of the church for the 21st century.

His life mission is to advance the Kingdom of God on earth by raising a generation of history makers who will live for a cause larger, bigger and greater than themselves. Those who will live like Jesus and transform every sphere of the society in every nation as a model of the Kingdom of God on earth.

His economic empowerment program has succeeded in raising over 200 millionaires in the short period of three years.

Sunday Adelaja is the author of over 300 books, many of which are translated into several languages including Russian, English, French, Chinese, German, etc.

His work has been widely reported by world media outlets such as The Washington Post, The Wall Street Journal, New York Times, Forbes, Associated Press, Reuters, CNN, BBC, German, Dutch and French national television stations.

Pastor Sunday is happily married to his "Princess" Bose Dere-Adelaja. They are blessed with three children: Perez, Zoe and Pearl.

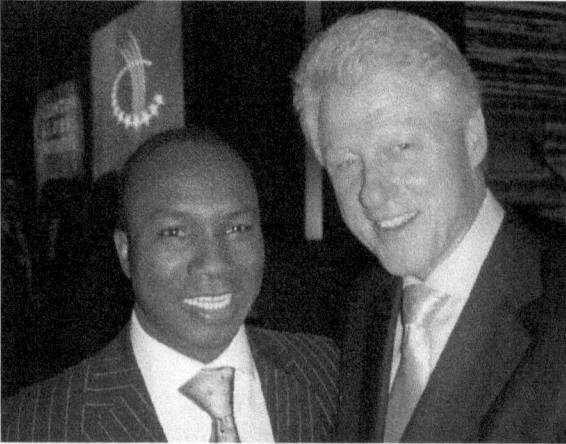

Bill Clinton —
42Nd President Of The
United States (1993–2001),
Former Arcansas State
Governor

Ariel "Arik" Sharon —
Israeli Politician, Israeli
Prime Minister (2001–2006)

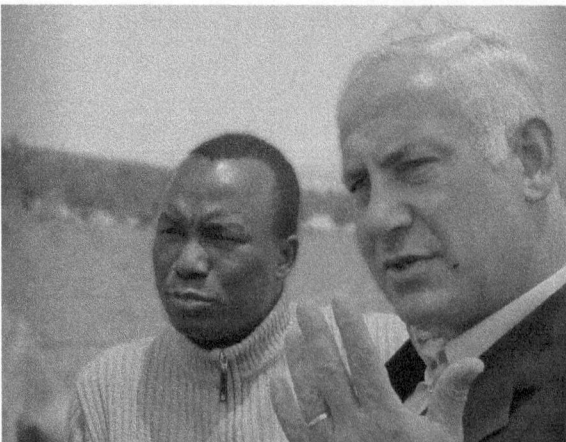

Benjamin Netanyahu —
Statesman Of Israel. Israeli
Prime Minister (1996–1999),
Acting Prime Minister
(From 2009)

Jean ChrEtien —
Canadian Politician,
20Th Prime Minister Of
Canada, Minister Of Justice
Of Canada, Head Of Liberan
Party Of Canada

Rudolph Giuliani —
American Political Actor,
Mayor Of New York Served
From 1994 To 2001. Actor
Of Republican Party

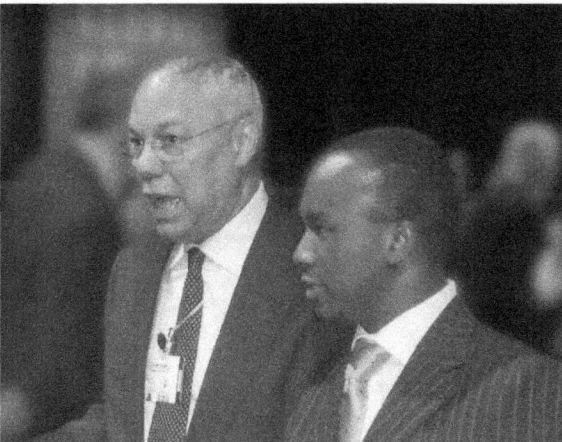

Colin Powell —
Is An American Statesman
And A Retired Four-Star
General In The Us Army,
65Th United States Secretary
Of State

Peter J. Daniels — Is A Well-Known And Respected Australian Christian International Business Statesman Of Substance

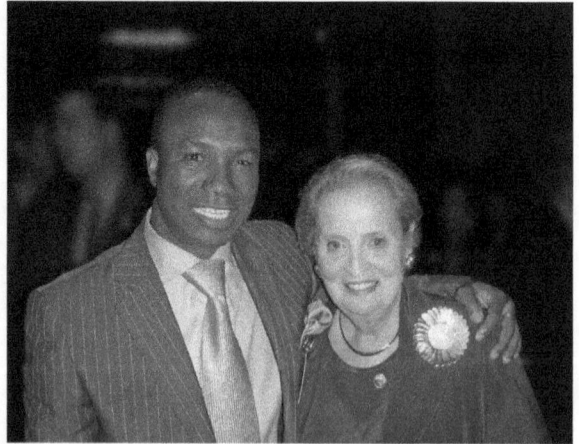

Madeleine Korbel Albright — An American Politician And Diplomat, 64[Th] United States Secretary Of State

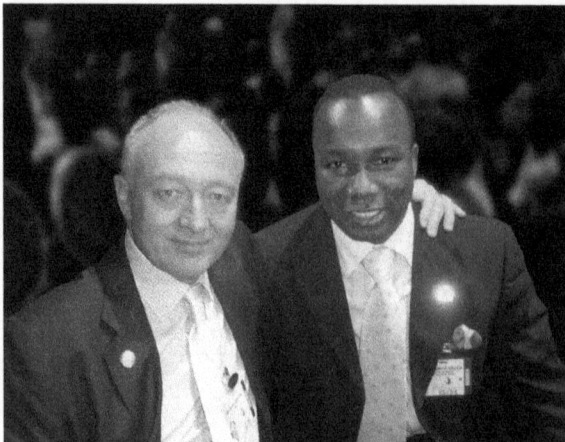

Kenneth Robert Livingstone — An English Politician, 1[St] Mayor Of London (4 May 2000 – 4 May 2008), Labour Party Representative

Sir Richard Charles Nicholas Branson —
English Business Magnate, Investor And Philanthropist. He Founded The *Virgin Group*, Which Controls More Than 400 Companies

Mel Gibson —
American Actor And Filmmaker

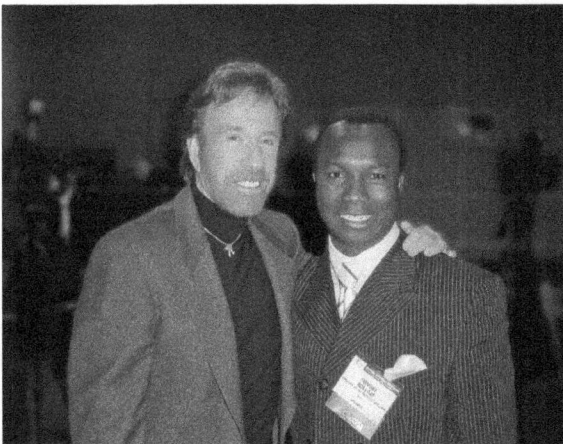

Chuck Norris —
American Martial Artist, Actor, Film Producer And Screenwriter

Christopher Tucker —
American Actor
And Comedian

Bernice Albertine King —
American Minister Best
Known As The Youngest
Child Of Civil Rights Leaders
Martin Luther King Jr. And
Coretta Scott King Andrew

Andrew Young — American
Politician, Diplomat, And
Activist, 14Th United States
Ambassador To The United
Nations, 55Th Mayor Of
Atlanta

General Wesley
Kanne Clark —
4-Star General And Nato
Supreme Allied Commander

Dr. Sunday Adelaja's family:
Perez, Pearl, Zoe and Pastor Bose Adelaja

FOLLOW
SUNDAY ADELAJA
ON SOCIAL MEDIA

Subscribe And Read Pastor Sunday's Blog:

www.sundayadelajablog.com

Follow these links and listen to over 200

of Pastor Sunday`s Messages free of charge:

http://sundayadelajablog.com/content/

Follow Pastor Sunday on Twitter:

www.twitter.com/official_pastor

Join Pastor Sunday's Facebook page to stay in touch:

www.facebook.com/pastor.

sunday.adelaja

Visit our websites for more

information about Pastor

Sunday's ministry:

http://www.godembassy.com

http://www.pastorsunday.com

http://sundayadelaja.de

CONTACT

FOR DISTRIBUTION OR TO ORDER
BULK COPIES OF THIS BOOK,
PLEASE CONTACT US:

USA

CORNERSTONE PUBLISHING

info@thecornerstonepublishers.com

+1 (516) 547-4999

www.thecornerstonepublishers.com

AFRICA

SUNDAY ADELAJA MEDIA LTD.

E-mail: btawolana@hotmail.com

+2348187518530, +2348097721451, +2348034093699

LONDON, UK

PASTOR ABRAHAM GREAT

abrahamagreat@gmail.com

+447711399828, +441908538141

KIEV, UKRAINE

pa@godembassy.org

Mobile: +380674401958

BEST SELLING BOOKS BY DR. SUNDAY ADELAJA
AVAILABLE ON AMAZON.COM AND OKADABOOKS.COM

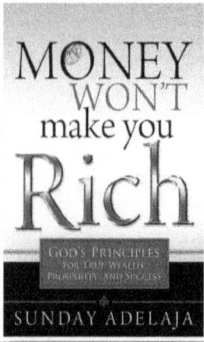

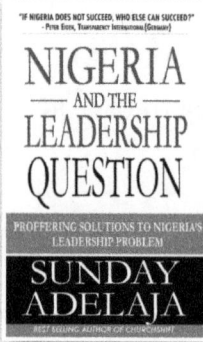

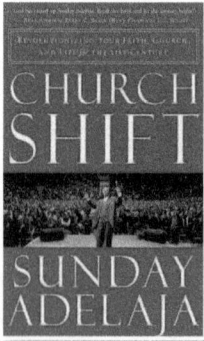

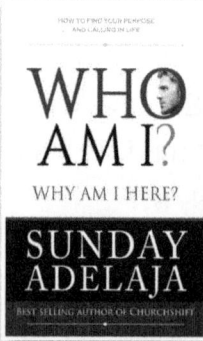

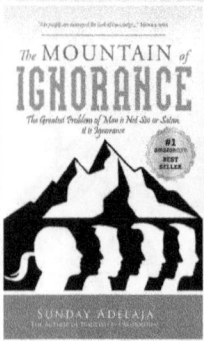

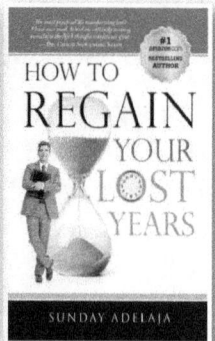

BEST SELLING BOOKS BY DR. SUNDAY ADELAJA
AVAILABLE ON AMAZON.COM AND OKADABOOKS.COM

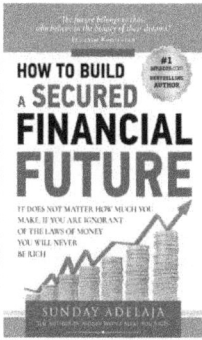

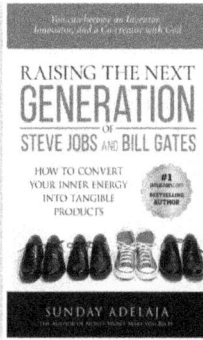

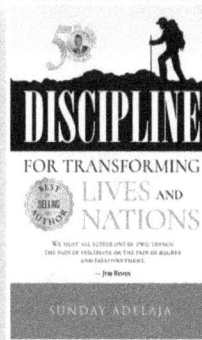

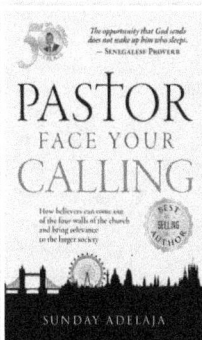

GOLDEN JUBILEE SERIES BOOKS
BY DR. SUNDAY ADELAJA

FOR DISTRIBUTION OR TO ORDER BULK COPIES OF THIS BOOKS, PLEASE CONTACT US:

USA | CORNERSTONE PUBLISHING
E-mail: info@thecornerstonepublishers.com, +1 (516) 547-4999
www.thecornerstonepublishers.com

AFRICA | SUNDAY ADELAJA MEDIA LTD.
E-mail: btawolana@hotmail.com
+2348187518530, +2348097721451, +2348034093699

LONDON, UK | PASTOR ABRAHAM GREAT
E-mail: abrahamagreat@gmail.com, +447711399828, +441908538141

KIEV, UKRAINE |
E-mail: pa@godembassy.org, Mobile: +380674401958

www.ingramcontent.com/pod-product-compliance
Lightning Source LLC
Chambersburg PA
CBHW031930190326
41519CB00007B/472